FACES OF UNION SOLDIERS
AT CULP'S HILL

Gettysburg's Critical Defense

JOSEPH STAHL & MATTHEW BORDERS

FOREWORD BY D. SCOTT HARTWIG

THE
History
PRESS

Published by The History Press
Charleston, SC
www.historypress.com

First published 2023

Manufactured in the United States

ISBN 9781467154406

Library of Congress Control Number: 2023932170

To the twenty-eight soldiers whose stories are contained within these pages.

CONTENTS

Breastworks of the 102nd New York Infantry of Greene's Brigade on Culp's Hill. *Library of Congress.*

FOREWORD

The orders for the Army of the Potomac's 12th Corps for July 1 were to march approximately five miles from Littlestown, Pennsylvania, to a tiny village known as Two Taverns, about five miles from the Adams County seat of Gettysburg. Here it could support the planned advance of the 1st and 11th Corps to the Gettysburg area.

The 12th Corps was something of a stepchild in the army. It had been created in March 1862, but its component units never operated together until the summer of 1862, when it was assigned to the newly formed Army of Virginia and designated as the 2nd Corps. The experience of the 2nd Manassas Campaign was an unhappy one for the corps, and at its conclusion, it was re-designated the 12th Corps and attached to the Army of the Potomac. Though understrength, it fought well at Antietam but was in such poor condition afterward that it was left to recover during the Fredericksburg Campaign.

The corps rejoined the main army for the Chancellorsville Campaign and again gave a good account of itself in fierce fighting. Since the fall of 1862, the corps was commanded by Major General Henry Slocum, a thirty-five-year-old West Point graduate from New York State. Slocum was competent but extremely cautious. At Gettysburg, he commanded two divisions with slightly over ten thousand men and an artillery brigade with twenty guns.

Slocum's troops completed their march to Two Taverns around noon. They heard heavy firing from the direction of Gettysburg, but Slocum hesitated to move. Even a message from 11th Corps commander, Major

General Oliver O. Howard, that they were in a severe battle at Gettysburg failed to budge Slocum, and it was not until 3:00 p.m. that the 12th Corps stirred and started for Gettysburg. When the troops reached the battlefield, the 2nd Division under Brigadier General John Geary was sent to hold the left of the forming Union front on the north slope of Little Round Top. Brigadier General Alpheus Williams's 1st Division moved to the right, nearly to the Hanover Road, before being recalled to the Baltimore Pike, near Rock Creek.

Major General George G. Meade, commanding the Army of the Potomac, ordered Slocum to move the 12th Corps into position on Culp's Hill the next morning, where it would anchor the right flank of the army and protect the vital Baltimore Turnpike, the army's main line of communications. The two divisions reached the hill early on July 2. Brigadier General James Wadsworth's 1st Corps division occupied the northwestern part of the hill and had built breastworks the night before. General Geary called together his brigade commanders and asked them their opinion of building breastworks, adding his view that he was opposed to the idea because it "unfitted men for fighting without them." Fortunately, Brigadier General George S. Greene, commanding the 3rd Brigade, replied that the saving of lives was of far more consequence than any theories about breastworks and that his men would have them. There was likely no question regarding breastworks for the soldiers of General Alpheus Williams's 1st Division. They had proven their value at Chancellorsville.

Soon, along the entire front of the corps, the men were hard at work gathering "sticks, stones, and chunks of wood," along with felled trees and shoveled earth to build a formidable line of breastworks from the summit of Culp's Hill to its base near Rock Creek. The photograph here by Mathew Brady, taken around July 15, shows the formidable nature of these works.

The day passed uneventfully for the corps until about 3:30 p.m. when the sounds of heavy fighting were heard from the army's left. At the same time, the summit of Culp's Hill and Cemetery Hill came under Confederate artillery fire, but no infantry attack developed; with pressure steadily increasing on his left, General Meade requested Slocum send all the men he could spare as reinforcements. Slocum ultimately decided to send his entire corps save one brigade, Greene's, of only 1,400 men, left to defend Culp's Hill.

No sooner had the bulk of the corps departed than Lieutenant General Richard Ewell's Confederate Second Corps opened an infantry attack on the Union right, sending an entire division, Major General Edward Johnson's, to seize Culp's Hill. Greene had stretched his line into a single rank to cover as much of the breastworks as he could, but nearly all of the 1st Division's works were unmanned. Captain George K. Collins of the 149th New York recalled "the pale faces, starting eye-balls, and nervous hands grasping loaded muskets" and the terrible suspense his men felt as the yelling Confederates surged up the hill. The battle raged with great fury on into the night, but the breastworks gave Greene's men excellent cover and the Confederates were checked across his front. Reinforcements from the 1st and 11th Corps arrived and bolstered Greene's defense.

On Greene's right, however, Johnson's Confederates seized most of the vacant works of the 1st Division. A decision was made to launch an attack at daylight July 3 to drive them out. The Confederates made a similar decision, with Ewell reinforcing Johnson and planning a daylight assault to capture Culp's Hill. The result was the longest sustained fighting at Gettysburg, from about 4:30 a.m. to 10:00 a.m. Repeated Confederate assaults failed to break through the entrenched Federals. Geary's 2nd Division alone fired 250,000 rounds of ammunition, offering a sense of the firepower employed. "The appearance of the men, as they worked in the trenches with their clothes ragged and dirty, their faces black from smoke, sweat and burnt powder, their lips cracked and bleeding from salt-petre in the cartridges bitten by them…resembled more the inhabitants of the bottomless pit," wrote Captain Collins.

By 10:00 a.m., the Confederates had broken off their attack and withdrawn, leaving behind hundreds of casualties. War is as unlike a sporting event as is possible, and there was no euphoria among the 12th Corps soldiers at their victory. "The impressions received during that morning [July 4] walk will never be effaced from memory. It made the men sick both in body and mind," recalled Captain Collins.

On July 5, the corps marched away from the battlefield to the relief of all "to rid themselves of the mud and stench" of the dismal field. In the pages of this book, you can look into the faces of those 12th Corps soldiers who lived this dreadful event, read their stories and remember the price paid to preserve the Union and destroy slavery in America.

—D. Scott Hartwig,
November 2022

ACKNOWLEDGEMENTS

The authors would like to thank the following individuals for their continued assistance and support in making *Faces of Union Soldiers at Culp's Hill: Gettysburg's Critical Defense* possible. First, we were thrilled to have the former supervisory historian of Gettysburg National Military Park, Scott Hartwig, write the foreword for the book and review some of the early chapters. His support of this type of research was very encouraging. As ever, our colleagues in the Antietam Battlefield Guides enthusiastically supported our research. Former chief of the Antietam guides Jim Rosebrock reviewed the manuscript, as did retired guide William Sagle, while Jim Buchanan was once again of great assistance in scanning and preparing the soldier CDVs for publication. Finally, the authors would like to thank The History Press for the opportunity to continue this series. *Faces of Union Soldiers at Culp's Hill: Gettysburg's Critical Defense* would not have been possible without Banks Smither, our acquisitions editor, who advocated on our behalf to The History Press.

Joe again had Dr. John Hiller review the manuscript, and his support continues to be greatly appreciated. Dr. Brad Gottfried's troop movement maps of the Gettysburg Battlefield were crucial to this work. Thank you, Brad, for again allowing the use of your fine maps and editing them as needed.

Matt's family and friends continue to support his passion for the American Civil War. Fellow 3rd Marylander Dave Bloom provided several important insights into the structure of that regiment in 1864. Matt's mother, Dr. Janet Borders, was particularly helpful in the genealogical research for this series. As ever, all my love.

List of Maps and Images

Introduction

CARTE DE VISITE (CDV)

Carte de visite is French for "visiting card." By 1860, these paper images had become common in the United States, as the price was within reach of many people ($2.50 to $3.00 per dozen). Due to this, it was not unusual to have an album of images of the family and relatives. The cameras of the era took four images from four lenses at one time. The glass negative could produce multiple copies, which accounted for the low price. The images were then pasted onto a piece of card to make them sturdier; this was done for all CDVs at the time, and a lack of a seam can be a good indicator when determining if an image is a modern reproduction. These images became very popular with soldiers, allowing them to show off their uniforms, leave a keepsake for someone at home or give a copy to a comrade. Some of the CDVs included in this work have a stamp on the back of them. From August 1, 1864, to August 1, 1866, the images were taxed by the federal government and required a revenue stamp on the reverse of the card (this helps in dating some cards). The tax was to help raise funds for the war effort: two cents on photographs under twenty-five cents, three cents on photos up to fifty cents and five cents for those costing up to a dollar. The tax stamps were to be canceled, to indicate that the tax was paid, usually by having a line drawn through the stamp with the photographer's initials and the date of the sale. Unfortunately, this regulation was often ignored and the stamps were either struck out or rubber-stamped for convenience.[1] Collecting images of the generals became popular during the war; as a result, many different poses of some generals exist and are available today. By the 1880s, other sizes of photographs had begun to replace the CDV in popularity.

We have also included a description of each soldier's image to discuss the details that can be made out in each CDV. Specifics such as uniform features, rank and other aspects of the images are discussed. It is hoped that these details will help readers see these men as the individuals they were and not just faded faces from a bygone era.

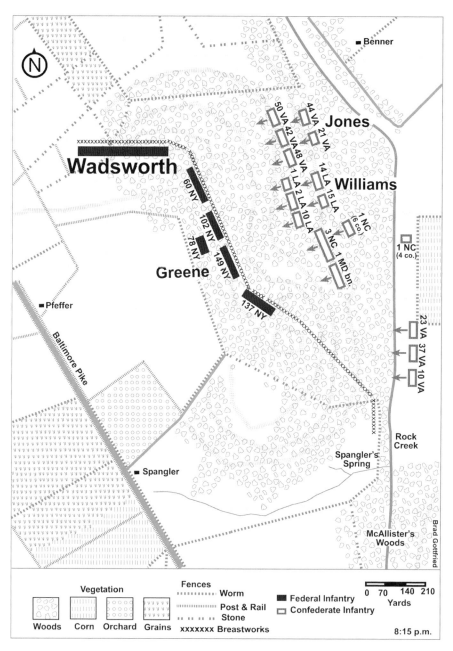

Brigadier General Greene's Brigade defends Culp's Hill.

Chapter 1

BRIGADIER GENERAL GEORGE SEARS GREENE'S BRIGADE

The "White Star Division," or the 2nd Division of the XII Corps, had been marching hard for days when it approached Gettysburg, Pennsylvania, around 5:00 p.m. on July 1. Commanded by Brigadier General John Geary, most of the division was first sent to the Federal left, to the base of Little Round Top, where they went into camp. Geary's Division was relieved by elements of the III Corps around 5:00 a.m. on July 2, at which point the men were marched to the Federal right at Culp's Hill. There they went into line on the top of Culp's Hill, with the I Corps to their left.

That evening, Brigadier General George Greene's 3rd Brigade of Geary's Division was deployed facing east on Culp's Hill. Greene's Brigade was positioned in the saddle between the two knobs of Culp's Hill. There the men dug in, preparing as strong a breastwork as possible from whatever they could find and the large boulders of the hill. The brigade consisted of five regiments from New York with a strength of 1,541 officers and enlisted men. The left end of the line was held by the 78th New York Infantry, whose men were later thrown forward as the skirmishers for the brigade. To their right was the 60th New York Infantry, followed by the 102nd New York and the 149th New York. The right end of the line was held by the 137th New York Infantry, whose men connected Greene's Brigade to the 2nd Brigade under Brigadier General Thomas Kane. Behind Greene, in support, was Colonel Charles Candy's 1st Brigade.[2] Both Kane and Candy's brigades were ordered south on the afternoon of July 2 to bolster the Federal left, with only Greene's Brigade of the XII Corps remaining on the east face of Culp's Hill.

78th New York Infantry

Known as the 78th Highlanders, the regiment was composed primarily of men from the New York City, Utica, Buffalo, Bath, China, Rochester and Suspension Bridge communities, while Company K was from Michigan. It was mustered into United States service in New York City from October 1, 1861, through April 12, 1862, for a three-year enlistment and left for Washington, D.C., on April 29.[3]

Initially assigned to the defenses of Washington, on May 25 the 78th New York Infantry was ordered to Harpers Ferry. There it remained until June 16, when the regiment was assigned to Major General Franz Sigel's Division in the Department of the Shenandoah. Ten days later, on June 26, it became a part of the 3rd Brigade, 2nd Division, II Corps, Army of Virginia. Interestingly, the 78th New York remained a part of this brigade and division for its entire service, through three different army corps and even three armies.[4]

Along with Major General John Pope's Army of Virginia, the 78th New York fought its first battle on August 9, 1862, at Cedar Mountain. The regiment continued with General Pope's forces through the Northern Virginia Campaign until assigned to the XII Corps of the Army of the Potomac on September 12, 1862. It saw limited action at Antietam on September 17 and was not involved with Fredericksburg that December due to the regiment guarding supplies. The 78th New York did take part in the infamous "Mud March" in January 1863 before settling into winter quarters.[5]

The following spring, the 78th New York suffered its greatest loss at Chancellorsville. Following the Federal defeat, the regiment took part in the race northward that resulted in the Battle of Gettysburg. There it was heavily engaged during the fighting on Culp's Hill. Following the pursuit of the Confederate Army of Northern Virginia that fall, the 78th New York, and the rest of the XII Corps, was ordered to Tennessee as part of the effort to relieve Federal forces besieged in Chattanooga. There it was assigned to the Army of the Cumberland and took part in the Chattanooga-Ringgold Campaign that fall before wintering around Chattanooga.[6]

By April 1864, the 78th New York had become part of the XX Corps, serving in Major General William T. Sherman's Military Division of the Mississippi during the Atlanta Campaign. Owing to its losses during this and earlier battles, the 78th New York was transferred to the 102nd New York on July 12, 1864. There it served through the rest of the Atlanta Campaign, the March to the Sea and the Carolinas Campaign before mustering out in July 1865.[7]

Lieutenant Colonel Herbert von Hammerstein wrote the after-action report for the 78th New York and described the desperate fighting on July 2 into July 3, 1863, as follows:

On the morning of the 2d, about 6 o'clock, my regiment took position on the left of the brigade, in line of battle, having the Sixtieth New York Volunteers on its right and the First Army Corps on its left. It covered part of the crest of a steep hill. A breastwork of trees and dirt was soon thrown up, and the day passed till about 4 o'clock without any incident. At about that time a battery of the enemy, numbering eight pieces, opened on a battery on our left, the shots passing our line without doing injury, when Battery K, Fifth U.S. Artillery, with two 10-pounder Parrott and two Napoleon guns, was at 4.30 o'clock ordered up to occupy the position which my regiment occupied and silence the rebel guns. I fell back a few yards to the rear of the battery, and remained there during the artillery contest.

At about 6 o'clock the battery was withdrawn, and, after reoccupying my old position, I received orders from Brig.-Gen. Greene to relieve the Twenty-eighth Pennsylvania Volunteers as skirmishers with my regiment. I at once marched the regiment down to the center of our brigade, crossed the breastworks, and deployed my skirmishers, not being able to see the Twenty-eighth Pennsylvania Volunteers, and having no time to look for them, as the enemy was already pressing all the skirmishers back. Our skirmishers came in soon, and, after giving and receiving some severe volleys of musketry, we fell back across the breastworks. The whole line behind the works was then occupied by our brigade, no interval existing. Gen. Greene ordered me to fall in, with my regiment in front of me, which I did. I joined the One hundred and second New York, and we, with the rest of the brigade, succeeded in repulsing a most furious attack of the enemy, beginning at 6.40 o'clock and ending at 9.30 o'clock, when the enemy fell back, and we fired our last round of ammunition.—Filling our boxes with ammunition, at 3.30 a.m. I received orders to occupy a place between the One hundred and second and Sixtieth Regt.'s, which was done immediately, and ten minutes afterward the attack began with the same energy which the rebels displayed on the evening before. Our men succeeded in repulsing them totally, with the same coolness and determination, before 6 a.m. At 7.40 o'clock my regiment was relieved by the One hundred and fiftieth New York Volunteers, to rest and clean their guns.

At 9 a.m. we reoccupied our old place, remaining there until 1 p.m., only annoyed by sharpshooters. At 1 o'clock we were relieved again. From 9 p.m. till 1 a.m. we were at the breastworks again.[8]

Sergeant Scott W. Skinner

One of those working behind the lines at Culp's Hill was Sergeant Scott W. Skinner from Company G of the 78th New York Volunteer. Born in Wheatland, New York, on June 16, 1844, Scott was seventeen when he enlisted in his hometown on December 16, 1861.[9] He was made a sergeant and mustered into Federal service on February 18, 1862, for a three-year enlistment. Scott was "present" until June 30, 1862, but was listed as "absent" from the company starting on October 8, 1862, when he was assigned to the Ambulance Corps. He remained with the Ambulance Corps until July 12, 1864, when he was transferred to Company G of the 102nd New York Infantry.[10] That same month, Scott was reported sick on his muster roll and present in the Division Hospital. He appears to have remained there for the rest of his service. Unfortunately, there is no specific sickness or hospital location listed. Scott was with the 102nd New York until the regiment mustered out on April 5, 1865, at Goldsboro, North Carolina. He, however, remained in the hospital until July 1865.[11]

Apparently inspired by his time in the Ambulance Corps, after the war Scott Skinner enrolled in Hahnemann Medical College of Philadelphia, where he graduated in 1868. He married that same year and in 1874 moved to Le Roy, New York, to begin a medical career of more than fifty years. During that period, Dr. Skinner served as the Genesee County coroner, and in 1889, he was appointed a pension examiner by President Benjamin Harrison. He was later made president of the Board of Examiners by President William McKinley.[12] An advocate of both Republicanism and education, Skinner organized the Le Roy Republicans League Club in 1880 and served as its president. He also supported the Le Roy Union School in 1890 and served as president of the Board of Education for years. Dr. Skinner was active in the Grand Army of the Republic, the Olive Branch Lodge of Masons and his church, St. Mark's Episcopal. On July 22, 1927, Dr. Scott Skinner passed away in his sleep at the age of eighty-three. He left behind three sons, two of whom were also doctors; his eldest was a lawyer. Dr. Skinner is buried at Machpelah Cemetery, Le Roy, New York.[13]

TAKEN BY THE POWELSON Gallery, likely at its Rochester, New York location due to its vicinity to Wheatland, this rather unusual CDV was probably captured at the beginning of Scott Skinner's service and used as a gift or

Left: Sergeant Scott Skinner, 78th New York Infantry. *Right*: Back of Skinner's image.

calling card, as he has signed the back "S.W. Skinner." The gallery provided a brace for Scott to lean against for the standing image; the base of the brace can be seen behind his feet. While CDVs did not require long exposures, especially in good lighting, the brace helped steady the head to make the subject's face as clear as possible in the final image.[14]

For the photo, it seems that the gallery may have provided most, if not all, of Scott Skinner's uniform. Starting at his shoes, these are in very good shape and are possibly civilian as opposed to issued. The toe appears to taper more than the enlisted man's brogans, while the smooth and thus polishable side of the leather is visible, as opposed to the rough out used by government manufacturers.[15] His trousers, while also appearing to be quite new, are sky-blue kersey wool with dark-blue piping along the seam. This had only become an option on December 16, 1861, with the issuance of General Orders #108, which stated, in part, that uniform trousers for both officers and enlisted men were to be sky-blue kersey wool, with dark-blue piping or stripes running down the seam to denote ranks.[16] Prior to this, trousers had been dark blue, with sky-blue piping. It is possible that these are his trousers and that the quartermaster of the 78th New York issued him two corporal's stripes to make up for a lack of sergeant's stripes for the pant legs. The stripes on Scott's left leg run parallel to each other with about a half-inch gap between. So with two half-inch corporal's stripes and a half inch between them, the one-and-a-half-inch stripe for a sergeant was achieved.[17]

The strangeness of Scott Skinner's uniform is particularly pronounced due to his frock coat. Although he is a sergeant, there is no indication of chevrons on this coat. Additionally, this frock, with its very long skirting and non-standard breast pocket, appears to be an officer's frock coat.[18] The frock is also very worn, its dark-blue color having faded significantly when compared to the dark-blue forage cap in Scott's hand. The frock coat also has only eight buttons, three of which are open, as opposed to the government-issued nine.[19] The buttons have the distinctive bulbous and ringed design of a state button, likely the New York Military Shield, although the detail is impossible to make out.[20] Around the waist of Scott's frock is his sword belt. Belts for both officers and noncommissioned officers were to be at least one and a half inches wide, made of plain black leather and secured by a two-inch rectangular belt plate. Scott's belt plate conforms to regulation, with its raised rim and the Arms of the United States, the eagle with wings spread, being visible in this image. Additional details—such as the silver laurel wreath around the eagle, the silver scroll containing the motto *E Pluribus Unum* and the silver stars—have all been washed out in this image.[21]

Attached to his sword belt are several slings, the first, running from the right shoulder to left hip, being an inch-wide shoulder strap meant to take some of the weight of the sword and scabbard. The scabbard is suspended by two additional slings, both of which are visible. These slings attached the scabbard to the belt by two suspension rings on the scabbard. The rings are attached to the topmost band on the scabbard, called the throat, and the middle band. The tip of the scabbard is covered by a sheath called the drag. The bands, drag and body of the scabbard are all likely bright iron, while the scabbard appears well used, with multiple dents.[22] The blade itself is an 1840 Light Artillery saber—the sweep of the blade, as well as its distinctive single-branch bronze guard, gives it away. The hilt has a Phrygian helmet pommel attached to a wooden grip wrapped with leather and wound with brass wire.[23] Altogether a curious weapon for an infantryman.

Scott has also included several personal items in his photo. As mentioned, in his right hand he holds his dark-blue forage cap, while on the ring finger of his left hand is a ring. In his breast pocket he has a handkerchief sticking out, and around his neck he has a new paper collar. Finally, Scott has combed his hair back, as well as neatly trimmed his beard and mustache to conform to regulations on proper grooming.[24]

60TH NEW YORK INFANTRY

The 60th New York Infantry, also known as the First St. Lawrence Regiment due to it being raised primarily in St. Lawrence County, New York, or the Ogdensburg Regiment, as it was organized at Ogdensburg, New York, was mustered into service on October 30, 1861, for three years.[25] The regiment left New York for Washington on November 4 and over the winter of 1861–62 served as part of Major General John Dix's Railroad Brigade, guarding the railways between Baltimore, Maryland, and the capital.[26] In June 1862, the regiment was assigned to Major General Franz Sigel's Division of the Department of the Shenandoah and later that month to the II Corps, Army of Virginia. With this command, the 60th New York participated in Major General John Pope's campaign. Following Pope's defeat and the opening of the Maryland Campaign, the regiment was assigned to the XII Corps of the Army of the Potomac on September 12. Five days later, at the Battle of Antietam, Colonel William Goodrich, formerly of the 60th New York and then commanding the brigade, was killed, and the regiment suffered significant losses. The 60th New York was fortunate to miss the Fredericksburg Campaign, as it was posted at Harpers Ferry, Virginia, with the XII Corps at the time. That December, the men were ordered south and went into winter quarters at Stafford Court House, Virginia.[27]

The following spring, the XII Corps led the advance of the Army of the Potomac during the Chancellorsville Campaign, where the 60th New York suffered its greatest casualties of the war. Two months later, at Gettysburg, its losses were again heavy in the defense of Culp's Hill on July 2–3, 1863.[28] The XII Corps was part of the pursuit of the Army of Northern Virginia, and by September, the 60th New York was picketing the Rapidan River near Raccoon Ford. It was there, on September 24, that the regiment was ordered to the Western Theater and after a circuitous route arrived at Bridgeport, Alabama, on October 27, 1863.[29]

The 60th New York was present at the Battle of Wauhatchie, Tennessee, at the end of October, as well as for the rest of the Chattanooga Campaign. The following spring, the regiment became a part of the XX Corps. It was with this command that the 60th New York fought through the Atlanta Campaign, the March to the Sea and the Carolinas. In June 1865, the regiment received veterans who had reenlisted and recruits from other regiments before being assigned to the XXII Corps, where it served until mustered out of the service at Alexandria, Virginia, on July 17, 1865.[30]

The part played by the 60th New York at Culp's Hill was reported by Colonel Abel Godard:

> On July 2, at or about 6 a.m., the regiment with the brigade assumed position in line of battle, connecting with the right of the First Army Corps, where my command threw up intrenchments, by order of Gen. Greene, in person commanding Third Brigade. The men of the regiment worked with a will until about 9 a.m., by that time completing the intrenchments. Our works connected on the right with those of the One hundred and second New York Volunteers, of our brigade. The line of the regiment was quiet until about 7 p.m., when the enemy's infantry advanced in force, our skirmishers falling back within our line, and we opened a fire upon the enemy's line, which continued along our whole line at close range, with, as was afterward discovered, terrible effect for about two hours, when, the firing of the enemy being nearly silenced, I ordered an advance of a portion of our regiment, who eagerly leaped the works and surrounded about 50 of the enemy, among whom were 2 officers, and took at the time two flags, one a brigade color and the other a regimental banner. At the receipt of these flags, a quiet enthusiasm pervaded the men and officers of the regiment.
>
> There was occasional firing by our regimental line until the break of day, July 3, when, with the exception of a reply to rebel sharpshooters, the firing ceased.
>
> The light firing above mentioned continued until a repeated advance of the enemy's infantry at about 4 a.m. July 3, when heavy firing opened on both sides, and continued until 9.30 a.m., the enemy being steadily held in check, at which time they retired, leaving only sharpshooters, who kept up interval firing until about 2 p.m., when my men being much exhausted, the Sixtieth were relieved for one hour, retiring from and returning to the intrenchments under a sharp fire of sharpshooters. Our men resumed their places behind the works about one hour after being first relieved, and then remained until 2 a.m. July 4, meanwhile there being no firing.[31]

Corporal Fred S. Winslow

On Culp's Hill, there is a separate monument to Company I of the 60th New York Infantry marking its position in front of the regiment. The members of the company are listed there, including Corporal Fred S. Winslow. Fred mustered into the 60th New York on October 30, 1861, as a private in Company I. He was twenty-one years old at the time and enlisted for three years.[32] His service records show that Fred was born in St. Lawrence, New York, and worked as a cooper before the war. According to the Company Descriptive Book, he had blue eyes, sandy hair, a florid complexion and was five feet, five and a half inches tall. On September 24, 1861, Fred was made a corporal prior to his muster-in date. In his records, he was listed as present starting in January/February 1862. On his February 1863 form is a note that he was at work on fortifications since February 11, 1863. That April, he was allowed to go on furlough for ten days to Ogdensburg, New York.[33] On December 24, 1863, Fred, with the majority of the 60th New York, reenlisted as a veteran regiment. Along with receiving veteran status, they received a reenlistment bonus and a thirty-day furlough home. During this reprieve from the war, Fred appears to have married.[34] At the time of his reenlistment, he had last been paid on August 31, 1863, and had drawn $59.29 against his clothing allowance. On June 1, 1864, Corporal Winslow was promoted to sergeant. The next note in his records states that on June 5, 1865, he was detailed as a regimental pioneer. Interestingly, near the end of his service, Fred was granted a fifteen-day furlough as of June 28, 1865. He returned to the 60th New York on July 16 and mustered out the next day in Alexandria, Virginia. Fred had last been paid on April 30 and since January 1 had drawn $39.03 against his clothing allowance; he also owed the government an additional $6.26 for unspecified reasons. Fortunately, he was still due $190 of his reenlistment bounty.[35]

After the war, Fred moved west, settling in Janesville, Wisconsin. For more than fifty years, he was an active participant in his community as a grocer, a father of four and a member of the G.W. Sargent Grand Army of the Republic Post No. 20.[36] Fred filed for a pension on October 7, 1904, and passed away on March 5, 1930, at Janesville, Wisconsin. Maria Winslow, his wife of sixty-six years, filed for a survivor's pension on March 17, 1930.[37] Fred Winslow remained in his adopted state and is buried in plot 054-03-8 at Oak Hill Cemetery in Janesville, Wisconsin.[38]

Left: Corporal Fred Winslow, 60ᵗʰ New York Infantry. *Right*: Back of Winslows' image.

THIS STANDING VIEW OF Fred Winslow was taken in Ogdensburg, New York, by photograper James M. Dow. The CDV was a gift, as it gives Fred's signature, "F.S. Winslow," along with "Presented to Miss Jan ____ of Brasher." While it is not known who the recipient was, they apparently lived in Brasher, New York, which is also in St. Lawrence County and had men in Company I of the 60ᵗʰ New York.[39] The photography studio provided Fred with a number of decorations for this image, including a carpet, a banister to brace himself on and, most obvious, a painted backdrop. These scenes could range from nature, such as the one here, to grand mansions and barns, libraries or even military or patriotic scenes.[40] The studio also provided a brace to steady his head; the base of it can be seen behind Fred's feet.

As for the image itself, it was taken at one of two points during Fred's service, either during his ten-day leave in April 1863 or, more likely, during his veterans' furlough in the winter of 1863–64. While the dark-blue trousers and lack of rank insignia suggest the beginning of the war, the presence of the white star, a corps badge, precludes that. The other significant clues to the possible date of this image are the condition of Fred's uniform and the card stock on which the image has been glued.

Fred is wearing the dark-blue trousers of the United States Army, which were standard before the Civil War. However, when the War Department issued General Orders #108, the uniform trousers for both officers and enlisted men was changed to sky-blue kersey wool, with dark-blue piping or stripes to denote ranks.[41] Even with this change, however, it was not uncommon to see dark-blue trousers being worn even late into the war. This was especially true with officers and those in the Regular Army, who used them to better differentiate themselves from the volunteer forces.[42]

Matching his trousers in color and beginning just above his knees is the skirting to Fred's dark-blue enlisted man's frock coat. Unlike that of the officers, the frock worn by the men in the ranks was much more form fitting. It also featured nine large federal eagle buttons, all of which can be seen here running down his front, and two small eagle buttons on each cuff. The frock may, as Fred's does, have piping to help indicate what branch of service the wearer is in. In this case, the infantry's sky-blue piping can be seen at the cuffs and around the collar.[43] There is no other indication of rank on either the frock or trousers, but Fred does have on his left breast a large white star, indicating the 2nd Division, XII Corps. The corps badges had been established by Major General Joseph Hooker on March 21, 1863. A specific symbol was given for each corps within the United States Army and a color to differentiate the divisions within the corps: red for the first division, white for the second and blue for the third. In the rare cases of a fourth division, green or yellow was used.[44]

While the frock coat has been hooked at the collar, it is unbuttoned, allowing for better ventilation and exposing Fred's civilian vest. Likely sky blue in color, the vest has more than a dozen round buttons, the majority of which can be seen and are unbuttoned. This, too, is likely for comfort or ventilation, but it also reveals Fred's white shirt. Halfway down his chest is a small tie or knot of some sort, the purpose or symbolism of which is unknown. The collar of the shirt can also be seen just above the collar of his frock. For this image, Fred has trimmed his mustache and combed back his hair. This keeps him well within regulations to keep any facial hair neat and trimmed.[45] A final piece of personal material can be found on the pinkie finger of his right hand, a ring. The ring is likely his wedding ring, as no tradition had yet been established to place the ring on a specific finger. It is quite possible that this image, if taken in the winter of 1864, was Fred's wedding picture. He was married in 1864, and his whole uniform in this image, down to his shoes, is extremely clean. Married or otherwise, Fred chose to look straight into the camera for this image. Now a veteran soldier, he knew exactly what he was headed back to in just a few short days.

First Lieutenant Eugene Diven

Also serving in the 60th New York Infantry was Eugene Diven of Company D. Born on June 21, 1843, in New York, Eugene was nineteen when he was commissioned a first lieutenant in Elmira, New York, on November 15, 1861.[46] Eugene's service records show that he was present with his regiment until January 5, 1863, when he was detached to serve as an "Aide to General [Nathaniel J.] Jackson." Not long after, on March 18, he requested a ten-day leave to return to Elmira, New York. On June 9, 1863, Lieutenant Diven was apparently back with the 60th New York and was transferred from Company D to Company B. The July/August report noted that Eugene was detached on July 23, 1863, and ordered to report to Major Alexander Diven, his father, then in Elmira, for temporary duty. He remained on detached duty until he was discharged on September 26, 1864, to be commissioned in the U.S. Volunteers Adjutant General Department with the rank of captain—the same department in which his father worked. The date of this transfer was recorded as either October 2 or October 15. Eugene remained a captain and assistant adjutant general for the rest of his service and resigned on April 5, 1865.[47]

While there is not much on Eugene Diven's postwar life besides that he married his wife, Julia, in 1869 and had a daughter, Vieva, in 1885, it appears that he stayed connected to his family in Elmira, New York.[48] Sadly, Eugene died on either August 30 or September 1 of 1888, he was just forty-five years old. No cause of death was listed in his pension record, and his wife did not apply for a survivor's pension until 1908. Interestingly, his sister-in-law died shortly after him on September 2, 1888. Both are buried with their respective spouses in the Diven family plot at Woodlawn Cemetery in Elmira.[49]

TAKEN IN ELMIRA, NEW YORK, by photographer W.J. Moulton, this standing image of Eugene Diven was likely a calling card or gift, as it is signed on the back with his name and hometown. Moulton provided a small stand or table but little else in the way of decoration for the shot. This is also true of

Left: Lieutenant Eugene Diven, 60th New York Infantry. *Right*: Back of Diven's image.

the photographer's advertisement: just a small eagle with flag on the back, with his name as well as two banners to provide the address. The image was likely taken in March 1863 or sometime that summer, as Eugene was home in Elmira during those periods and a first lieutenant at the time.

Wanting to look his best for the image, Eugene Diven's unique attire is a fine example of officers purchasing their own uniforms. His trousers are the dark-blue officer's trousers of the prewar army; the sky-blue piping signifying an infantry officer can be seen running down the seam of his right leg. Most striking, however, is his dark-blue, nine-button uniform jacket. The uniform jacket was a formal version of the short fatigue jacket known as a roundabout or shell jacket. Cut longer, this jacket included piping for the branch of service—in this case the trim along the collar and along the edges would be sky blue for the infantry.[50] The buttons on this uniform jacket cannot be determined but appear to be quite large and could be either New York Military Shield buttons or staff officers' buttons. There are also three smaller buttons along Eugene's right cuff. Adorning his cuffs are the most striking decoration on his jacket: the loop á echelle in gold braid. This can be seen on both sleeves but most prominently on the right. The braid was another form of identifying rank, but it was not one often seen on Federal uniforms beyond the overcoat, where it was a black silk cord. In this case, the single gold braid with one loop or knot signified a first lieutenant, with more braid and loops the higher the rank.[51] Interestingly, this gold lacing on an officer's sleeve was quite popular with Confederate officers. For Federal officers, the much more common symbol of rank, the shoulder boards, can also be seen. The gold embroidered border surrounds a dark-blue field with a single gold bar at each end, the rank of a first lieutenant staff officer.[52]

In Eugene Diven's left hand, resting slightly on the provided stand, is his slouch hat. A comfortable felt hat worn by many officers and enlisted men throughout the Civil War, the high crown and silk binding are clearly visible in this image, as is his officer's hat cord of black silk and gold, which can be seen circling the crown. The hat cord's two acorn finials can also be seen.[53] With his head uncovered for the image, Eugene has also combed his dark hair and has trimmed his mustache and goatee to conform to regulations and look his best.

102ND New York Infantry

The 102nd New York Infantry, also known as the Van Buren Light Infantry, was primarily recruited at New York City and named after its colonel, Thomas B. Van Buren. The regiment was completed by adding two companies from the 78th New York Infantry and Company A of the 12th Militia. With these additions, the 102nd New York was mustered into Federal service from November 1861 through April 1862.[54]

The 102nd New York left New York on March 10, 1862, and was assigned to the II Corps, Army of Virginia, with which it fought its first and most costly engagement at Cedar Mountain on August 9, 1862. The regiment remained with the Army of Virginia and fought with it at Second Bull Run. Following the Union defeat and retreat to Washington, the II Corps was transferred to the Army of the Potomac and reorganized as the XII Corps. As such, the 102nd New York was actively engaged at Antietam but avoided the Fredericksburg Campaign, as the XII Corps was guarding Harpers Ferry. At the end of 1862, the 102nd New York went into winter quarters at Stafford Court House, Virginia.

The following spring, the 102nd New York, as part of the White Star Division, fought hard at Chancellorsville, where it again lost heavily. Just two months later at Gettysburg, the regiment helped hold the Federal right at Culp's Hill. After pursuing the Confederate army south, the XII Corps left Virginia in September 1863 and joined Major General Ulysses S. Grant's forces outside Chattanooga, Tennessee. In the month following its arrival, the regiment was engaged in the Battle at Wauhatchie and later fought at Lookout Mountain in the Battle Above the Clouds.[55]

In the spring of 1864, the 102nd New York became part of the XX Corps. Under this new designation, the regiment fought through the Atlanta Campaign and the intense fighting in northern Georgia that entailed. In July 1864, the regiment received by transfer the officers and men of the 78th New York Infantry who had not reenlisted.[56]

Following the Fall of Atlanta, the 102nd New York took part in the March to the Sea and the final campaign in the Carolinas. The regiment was finally mustered out on July 21, 1865, at Alexandria, Virginia. Its division commander, Major General John W. Geary, complimented the regiment, stating, "It may safely be asserted that no organization in the army has a prouder record, or has passed through more arduous, varied and bloody campaigns."[57]

After the Battle of Gettysburg, the 102nd New York's official report was written by Captain Lewis R. Stegman, stating:

The division being moved to the right of the army, the One hundred and second New York was formed in line upon the side of a precipitous hill; the One hundred and forty-ninth New York upon the right, and the Sixtieth New York upon the left. Skirmisher and pickets from the First Corps occupied our front, but were relieved by detail. The men were ordered to build breastworks, and did so with the best material at hand—cord-wood and rock—making, however, a strong line.—Shortly after 6 p.m. the regiment was moved by the right flank to the intrenchments occupied by the One hundred and forty-ninth New York, the men forming in single file, with intervening spaces of a foot or more. The men had scarcely taken this position when some sharp musketry firing took place, proving an advance of the enemy and causing our pickets to retire. The Seventy-eighth New York, was dispatched through our lines to their relief, bravely led by Lieut.-Col. Hammerstein. The blaze of fire which lighted up the darkness of the valley below us; the desperate charging yell and halloa of the rebel troops, convinced us of an immediate engagement.

The men were cheered by their officers, continued to be on the alert, and to allow our pickets to pass.

The Seventy-eighth soon fell back in good order before the heavy columns of the foe, forming on the rear of our right wing, where they remained during the battle, relieving our men and in turn being relieved, fighting desperately and bravely. The pickets having crossed the breastworks, the whistling of the balls announce the advance of the enemy to close quarters. It was answered by volley after volley of the most destructive musketry from our regiment, being unceasing for two hours.

About 8 p.m. the right wing was re-enforced. The One hundred and second New York never left its position, nor did one man flinch from his full duty. The firing ceased along the line about 9.30 p.m.—At 3.30 a.m. the engagement recommenced with renewed intensity, this regiment holding the breastworks until nearly 9 a.m., in the face of a fearfully destructive fire, when they were relieved by the One hundred and fiftieth New York Volunteers. In about twenty minutes the regiment relieved the One hundred and fiftieth New York. About an hour thereafter the regiment was again relieved by the One hundred and fiftieth New York. They had scarcely formed near brigade headquarters when the First Maryland Regt. retired from the trenches without orders, and the One hundred and second New York was ordered to the position left vacant. Under a heavy fire from sharpshooters, they occupied this position until 2 p.m., when they were relieved by the Sixtieth New York Volunteers. About 4 p.m. this regiment was ordered to report to Brig.-Gen. Wadsworth, First Corps, by whom they were placed in reserve to his left wing, but in position to be used at any point in the line.[58]

Major Gilbert Malleson Elliott

Helping keep the 102nd New York armed throughout the fighting at Culp's Hill was Major Gilbert M. Elliott. Born in Thompson, Connecticut, in 1840, Gilbert Elliott had wanted nothing more than to follow his elder brother into higher education. By 1861, he had graduated valedictorian from the New York Free Academy and was teaching at Grammar School no. 53 prior to joining the 102nd New York Infantry. He enlisted in New York City as a first lieutenant in Company E on October 31, 1861. He was twenty-one years old at the time and had dreams of becoming a lawyer after the war.[59] His service records show that he was "present" from his muster into the service until July 15, 1862, when he was left at Front Royal, Virginia, due to sickness. Gilbert was detached from the 102nd New York on September 26, 1862, to be the division ordnance officer, and he was reported to be in Harpers Ferry, Virginia, in October. On November 15, 1862, Elliott was promoted to captain of Company H. He remained the division ordnance officer until February 28, 1863, and on March 4 was granted a ten-day leave of absence. Shortly after his return, he was promoted again to major on March 18, 1863, effective as of July 17, 1863.[60] Having been appointed chief of ordnance in May, during the Battle of Gettysburg Gilbert was said to have "received orders, issued stores, and filed vouchers while the conflict was raging, with as much coolness as a clerk in a city store."[61]

By July 31, 1863, Gilbert Elliott was in command of the 102nd New York.[62] He remained present for duty throughout the transfer of the XII Corps to the Western Theater and took part in the opening battles to relieve Chattanooga. Sadly, on November 24, 1863, Major Gilbert Elliott was killed during the assault on Lookout Mountain. Gilbert had corresponded frequently with his younger brother James Elliot during his service, and it was James who received word from Surgeon Charles H. Lord of the 102nd New York of his brother's passing. Surgeon Lord described how Gilbert led his regiment in the attack on Lookout Mountain and was cut down by a sharpshooter. Borne from the field by his men, Gilbert apparently suffered little, his last words being, "Tell my family I died like a brave man." His effects were gathered and with his remains sent back to New York, arriving there on December 7, 1863.[63] For his service, Gilbert was awarded brevet promotions to lieutenant colonel for "Gallant & Meritorious Service at the Battle of Chancellorsville, Virginia" and to colonel for service at Lookout Mountain. Both brevets were dated March 13, 1865.[64] As he was deeply lamented by his friends, particularly his classmates from the New York Free Academy, a committee was formed on December 5, 1863, with its commemorative resolutions published as an obituary on December 10: "[W]e are for the first time since our graduation called upon to give expression to our deep sorrow for the loss of one who was an esteemed and worthy classmate, an intelligent and accomplished scholar, a faithful and agreeable friend, and in whom we recognized the upright and respected citizen, the heroic and successful soldier, the dutiful son and affectionate brother."[65] After a moving service at the Pilgrim Baptist Church, Gilbert Elliott was buried in the village of Morrisania, New York.[66] After the war, his mother filed for a survivor's pension on April 24, 1887.[67]

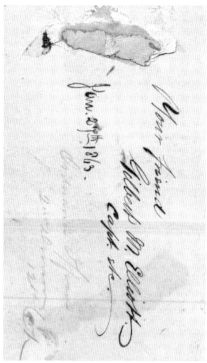

Left: Lieutenant Gilbert Elliott, 102ⁿᵈ New York Infantry. *Right*: Back of Elliott's image.

THIS IMAGE OF GILBERT Elliott, standing bare-headed and wearing his spectacles, was taken a few months after his promotion to captain but while he was still the 2ⁿᵈ Division, XII Corps ordnance officer. The image has no advertiser's mark or photographer's stamp on the back and appears to have been removed from an album at some point. This was also a gift, as it has been signed, "Your friend Gilbert M. Elliott, Capt. etc." Elliott has even recorded the date, January 24, 1863. He remained the ordnance officer until February, and there is a note in pencil under his signature: "Ordnance Officer 2ⁿᵈ Division 12ᵗʰ Corps."

In the picture, Gilbert stands on a patterned floor before a prop banister, which was being used as a brace and includes a stand for his kepi. Encasing Gilbert's legs is a pair of impressively tall, soft leather boots. Called a "top boot," these were designed to be pulled up over the knee.[68] Beginning just above the top of his boots is Gilbert's dark-blue officer's frock. The extra-long skirting, voluminous sleeves, velvet collar and the three buttons on the left cuff give the coat away as an officer's garment. Of the nine officer's buttons running down the front, eight are visible; the ninth is likely under his sash and sword belt. Gilbert's shoulder boards sit prominently on his shoulders, the sky blue of an infantry officer clearly visible within the gold embroidered border, although the image is too washed out to see his captain's bars.

Around Gilbert Elliot's waist is his crimson silk net sash. Although the sash was supposed to be wrapped twice around the body and tied behind the left hip, the bullion fringes have been shifted forward of Gilbert's hip, likely to add more decoration to the image. Over the top of the sash, and helping to keep it in place, is his sword belt. Designed to be not less than one and a half inches wide and made of black leather, the belt also has two leather slings attached to it to help secure the sword. Fastening the belt is a two-inch-wide belt plate with a raised rim containing the Arms of the United States and the motto *E Pluribus Unum*. In this case, the belt plate has been washed out so that only the outline of the eagle and the raised rim can be seen.[69] Hanging off the belt's suspension hook is Gilbert's sheathed sword, with the leather slings attached to the suspension rings on the scabbard. These rings are located on the uppermost brass band of the scabbard, the throat, and the middle band, while the end of the scabbard is protected by a brass drag. The dark color of this scabbard suggests that it is made of black leather as opposed to a polished metal. Though sheathed, the sword itself appears to be a Model 1860 staff and field officer's sword, with its straight blade, single branch guard and kidney-shaped counter guard all visible. The wooden fish skin–wrapped grip is capped with a Phrygian helmet pommel, much like the Model 1850, and the gold lace strap with bullion tassel sword knot can be seen wrapped around the guard.[70]

Finally, sitting on its own stand is Gilbert Elliot's officer's kepi. Based off a French design, the kepi was a short cap with a leather bill and a black leather chin strap. The crown of the cap is counter sunk, as can be seen here, and the kepi could be heavily decorated with braid depending on the desire of the owner. In this case, Gilbert went with a very simple kepi—the only decoration is the symbol of the infantry, the hunter's horn. This gold embroidered horn sits on a black felt patch that has been sewn to the front of the kepi. In the loop of the horn can be seen the silver number "102" for the 102nd New York Infantry.[71] With his hair swept back and his mustache neatly trimmed, Gilbert looks ready to take on the responsibilities of his new rank and those that followed him.

Captain Barent Van Buren

There were many famous names among the combatants at Gettysburg, including those who fought at Culp's Hill. One such individual was Barent Van Buren, the second cousin of President Martin Van Buren, born on March 8, 1840, in Orange County, New York. A clerk at a New York drugstore before the war, Barent enlisted in the 102nd New York Infantry on December 23, 1861.[72] Upon mustering into service, he was commissioned on March 7, 1862, as the second lieutenant of Company F. He was promoted to first lieutenant on August 9, 1862, and transferred to Company H. He remained present for duty until September 14, 1862, when he became sick and was absent from his regiment for two months. On November 13, 1862, Barent received a medical certificate that recommended a leave of thirty days. He requested a longer leave of eight to ten weeks but was only granted twenty days. Apparently still ill on December 15, 1862, he asked for an extension to his medical leave that was approved. When exactly he returned to the 102nd New York is not clear, but he was promoted on January 1, 1863, to captain of Company A. Barent had apparently been acting as a company commander for some time, as his records noted that he was due an extra ten dollars per month as a company commander from August to January 1, 1863. This note continues to be in his records through September 1864.

With command came additional responsibilities, and Barent Van Buren apparently had issues with misplacing company equipment. During the March/April 1864 period, he was charged $8.05 for "ordnance stores lost; 6 screw drivers, 2 spring vices, 5 wipers, 1 bayonet scabbard, 2 cap pouches, 2 cart boxes, 2 cart box belts and 2 waist belts plates." Four months later, he was again charged for "30 brass letters lost and 120 brass numbers lost"; the cost, however, was not shown. On December 27, 1864, Barent was discharged, as his term had expired. His muster-out form at Savannah, Georgia, noted that "10 days allowed to reach the place of general rendezvous and the Quartermaster Department will furnish transportation to New York City."[73] Barent's service to the nation, however, was not over, for on March 14, 1865, he was commissioned lieutenant colonel of the 192nd New York Infantry, with which he served until his muster out on August 28, 1865, at Cumberland, Maryland.[74]

After the war, Barent Van Buren returned to the drug business in New York. He later moved to Le Mont, Illinois, and finally in 1874 to Chicago, Illinois, where he opened a drugstore. He expanded his business in 1885 by building the Van Buren Block, which included a drugstore, paint shop

Left: Captain Barent Van Buren, 102nd New York Infantry. *Right*: Back of Van Buren's image.

and hardware store. Barent married Mildred Bader in 1894, and together they had four sons, only one of whom survived to adulthood.[75] Just a few weeks after his eldest was born, Barent filed for a pension on November 17, 1897.[76] An active member of his community, Barent was in numerous social organizations, including the Grand Army of the Republic. He retired from business on August 1, 1901, and passed away almost twenty years later, on April 22, 1921, in Chicago. He was buried at Forest Home Cemetery in Forest Park, Illinois.[77]

THIS CDV WAS TAKEN at the studio of Charles D. Fredericks in New York City; a previous collector has listed not only Barent Van Buren's name, rank and regiment but also the dates of his various promotions on the back of the image. This was likely either a gift or calling card, as Barent himself has signed the back, "Compliments of Capt. B Van Buren 102 NYV." Most intriguing, though, is the date that has been scrawled on the back, April 16, possibly 1863 or 1883. While it is possible that this was done while Barent was on sick leave in early 1863, it is also possible that that is a reprint, as photographers kept the glass plate negatives for that very reason.[78]

This standing view of Barent Van Buren has him bracing on a balustrade provided by the photography studio. Though cut off at about the knee, his dark-blue officer's trousers, with the eighth-of-an-inch sky-blue piping running along the seam, can be seen on his left leg. He is also wearing his nine-button officer's frock coat, its long skirting coming almost to the knee and six of the nine large general service buttons visible. Three buttons have been undone, likely for ventilation, and a large handkerchief can be seen coming from inside the coat; this was likely in the internal breast pocket. A small chain, perhaps for a watch, can be seen looping through the fourth buttonhole and back into that same internal pocket. This frock also has a short velvet collar, which was very popular with these private purchase officer coats, as well as a new, crisp paper collar.

Dominating his attire, however, is his dark-blue or black overcoat. This coat was designed to go over the top of the rest of the uniform for use in inclement weather or as an extra layer. While it is lacking the black silk loops, instead opting for buttons to close the coat, the large cape with sky-blue lining, falling collar and half-inch black silk braid along all the edges suggests that this is an officer's cloak coat.[79] While Barent Van Buren has made himself slightly less conspicuous by not including the knot and braiding on the cuffs used to distinguish rank, he has chosen to forgo General Orders #102, which allowed officers to wear the same sky-blue greatcoats as the enlisted men.[80]

In his right hand, Barent Van Buren holds a variation of the 1858 forage cap. This light cap with leather bill and chin strap has an infantry officer's patch on its front, a gold embroidered hunter's horn on a black velvet background. The patch appears to be edged in gold as well. In the loop of the horn can be seen Barent's regimental number, "102," picked out in silver.[81] As a final touch, Barent has combed his hair, mustache and mutton chops to look his best for the image.

137TH NEW YORK INFANTRY

The 137th New York Infantry was recruited in the 24th Congressional District of New York, which included the counties of Tompkins, Tioga and Broome. The regiment was organized at Binghamton, New York, at Camp Susquehanna and was mustered into United States service for three years on September 25–26, 1862.[82] The 137th New York left the state the next day, 1,007 strong, and was sent to Harpers Ferry, Virginia, by way of Washington and Frederick, Maryland. The regiment was assigned to the XII Corps, with which it remained attached until the XX Corps was formed in the spring of 1864.[83]

The 137th New York remained on Bolivar Heights, above Harpers Ferry, for most of the fall and early winter of 1862, where its men suffered severely from typhoid fever. A series of marches and skirmishes in late December and January meant that the regiment did not go into winter quarters near Aquia Creek Landing until February 7, 1863. It made its white stars, for the 2nd Division, XII Corps, in late April and were under fire at Chancellorsville that May. After the battle, the 137th New York returned to Aquia Landing, remaining there until June 13, when it began marching north in pursuit of Confederate forces, leading to the Battle of Gettysburg.[84] There, on Culp's Hill, the 137th New York paid for its tenacity defending the Federal right with blood.

In September, the 137th New York was sent west with the rest of the XII Corps and shared in all the marches and battles of the Atlanta Campaign. After Atlanta fell, its commander, Colonel David Ireland, succumbed to disease, and Colonel Koert S. Van Voorhes succeeded in command. The regiment then marched to the sea and through the Carolinas. With the surrender of Confederate General Joseph Johnston, the 137th New York returned to Washington, where it participated in the Grand Review and was mustered out near Bladensburg, Maryland, on June 9, 1865.[85]

The commander of the 137th New York, Colonel David Ireland, wrote of his regiment at Culp's Hill:

Early on the morning of Thursday, July 2, we marched from the position on the left to a position on the right of the road to Gettysburg and parallel to it. In this position we constructed a line of breastworks covering the front of the regiment. The breastworks were completed about noon. We marched in them and remained there until about 6 p.m., when I received orders to send out a company of skirmishers.—At the same time we were ordered to change our position to the line of works constructed by Gen. Kane's brigade, to occupy which we had to from line one man deep. In this position the right of our regiment was entirely unprotected. About 7 p.m. our skirmishers were driven in by the enemy, who were advancing in force, and, as near as I could see, in three lines. We remained in this position fighting the enemy until about 7.30 o'clock, when the enemy advanced on our right flank. At this time I ordered Company A, the right-flank company, to form at right angles with the breastworks, and check the advance of the enemy and they did for some time, but, being sorely pressed, they fell back a short distance to a better position, and there remained until Lieut. Cantine, of Gen. Greene's staff, brought a regiment of the First Corps. I placed them in the position occupied by Company A, but they remained there but a short time. They fell back to the line of works constructed by the Third Brigade. At this time we were being fired on heavily from three sides—from the front of the works, from the right, and from a stone wall in our rear. Here we lost severely in killed and wounded. At this time I ordered the regiment back to the line of works of the Third Brigade, and formed line on the prolongation of the works, and there held the enemy in check until relieved by the Fourteenth New York Volunteers. While in this position, and previous to being relieved, Capt. Gregg, in command of a small squad of men, charged with the bayonet the enemy that were harassing us most, and fell, mortally wounded, leading and cheering on his men. When relieved by the Fourteenth New York, we formed line in their rear, and in that position remained during the night. At 3 a.m of Friday, July 3, we relieved the One hundred and forty-seventh New York Volunteers in the breastworks, and at 4 a.m. the enemy advanced with a yell and opened on us. Their fire was returned, and kept up unceasingly until 5.45 o'clock, when we were relieved in splendid style by the Twenty-ninth Ohio Volunteers. We relieved them at 7 a.m., and were relieved again at 9.30 a.m. We relieved the Twenty-ninth Ohio again about 10.15 a.m. We were there but a short time when the fire slackened, and we retired a short distance, when the men rested and cleaned their arms.[86]

Private William A. Scofield

Likely assisting Brigadier General George S. Greene during the fighting at Culp's Hill was William A. Scofield. On September 3, 1862, twenty-two-year-old William mustered into Company F of the 137th New York Volunteer Infantry as a private. Born in Butternut, New York, William was described as five feet, eight and a half inches tall, with a fair complexion, blue eyes and brown hair; he was working on the railroad before he enlisted. Shortly after his muster, on October 16, 1862, William was detailed as a clerk at brigade headquarters and did not return to the 137th New York until sometime in November 1863.[87] He was likely utilized as a courier during the Battle of Gettysburg.

His efforts at brigade headquarters, however, earned him a promotion on December 4, 1863, to sergeant major of the regiment and a transfer to the field and staff. William returned to Company F on March 1, 1864, when he was promoted again to first lieutenant. At that time, he had last been paid on December 31, 1863, and had drawn $21.91 against his clothing allowance. During May–June 1864, now Lieutenant Scofield was detailed as aide-de-camp to Colonel David Ireland, then commanding the brigade. Now an officer, William had significantly more freedom to request leave, and on September 11, 1864, he requested and received a leave of twenty days to attend the funeral of his commander, Colonel Ireland, back in New York. William mustered out at Bladensburg, Maryland, on June 9, 1865. He was last paid on June 30, 1864, and was due three months' pay as sergeant major in addition to extra pay for having commanded Company A for a time.[88]

For his service, William Scofield was brevetted to captain in 1868 and returned to the railroad business after the war.[89] By 1870, he had married his wife, Antonette, and was working as a clerk in the railroad office in Hornellsville, New York.[90] Their daughter, Mary, was born in about 1871, and by 1875, the family were listed as living with Antonette's father in Union, New York, where William worked as a railroad conductor.[91] While no information regarding William's death or burial has been found, he could not be found in the 1880 census, and Antonette filed for a survivor's pension on September 18, 1883.[92]

WITH NO BACK MARK on the image, it makes it difficult to determine when this CDV was taken. It was obviously a gift, however, as William has inscribed the back with the greeting "Yours Truly," as well as his full signature, rank and command. Two clues in this signature help narrow down when the image was taken. First, the rank of first lieutenant places this image sometime after his return to the 137th New York in March 1864. Second, the reference to the XX Corps means that this was taken after the merger of the XI and XII Corps in April 1864. This image also lacks a tax stamp on the back, which would have been there if he had this taken when he returned home for Colonel Ireland's funeral in September. The tax stamps went into effect as a luxury tax to help pay for the war in August 1864 and were not rescinded until August 1866.[93]

Although this is a bust view, there are still a number of uniform details visible in this image. The first is William Scofield's dark-blue officer's frock. Three of the coat's nine buttons are visible, and the bulbous design with ring

Left: Private William Scofield, 137th New York Infantry. *Right*: Back of Scofield's image.

suggests either a New York Military Shield button or, just as likely due to his time as a staff officer, a staff officer's button.[94] Both of William's shoulder boards can be seen; the gold embroidered bar of a first lieutenant is just visible on the left shoulder. A black velvet collar encloses William's neck, while at the collar, just above the first button, is a non-regulation cravat. This cravat, enclosed by a new paper collar, appears to be blue with white polka dots or stars on it as opposed to the regulation black.[95] William has left his thick hair relatively uncombed but has trimmed his mustache for the shot. Standing with the slightest of smiles, William Scofield gazes off into the middle distance with a confident look.

Second Lieutenant George W.P. Pew

Among the men of Company H, 137th New York Infantry, on Culp's Hill was a second lieutenant named George W.P. Pew, born on October 24, 1831, in Ithaca, New York.[96] The thirty-one-year-old farmer had married Mary

C. Dodge in 1858, and together they had at least eight children over the course of their marriage.[97] However, on August 21, 1862, George enlisted at Spencer, New York, in the 137th New York and mustered into service as a sergeant on September 3, 1862. The Company Descriptive Book states that George was six feet, one inch tall, with a light complexion and blue eyes. Starting with the September 25, 1862 report, his service records show George as "present" until April 23, 1863, when he was sent home on a ten-day furlough. Before that, George had been promoted to first sergeant on February 12, 1863, and transferred to the field and staff. That spring, on May 23, George was promoted to second lieutenant of Company C. Just before the end of 1863, George received his final promotion to first lieutenant on December 2. During this period, although he was receiving portions of his enlistment bounty, he had last been paid on August 31, 1863. He had also drawn $61.76 against his clothing allowance, likely due to the cost of supplying his own officer's uniform. George was transferred to Company F and on January 15, 1864, applied for sick leave. This being approved, his leave began on January 29, and he returned to the regiment on February 23, 1864. Starting in the January/February report is a note that "extra pay due as Commander of Co. I from Dec 4 for responsibility of arms and clothing." That summer, Lieutenant Pew became sick again on June 23, 1864, and was absent until July 12. Late in his service, George was granted another leave of thirty days beginning on March 27, 1865, to return home to stay with one of his children, who needed to have an operation on their ankle. While his records fail to note when he returned to the 137th New York, he was mustered out of the service on June 9, 1865, in Bladensburg, Maryland, with the rest of the regiment.[98]

At some point after the war, George Pew and his family went west to Helena, Montana, and may have gotten involved in short horn cattle breeding.[99] He filed for a pension on July 21, 1890, which was increased to twelve dollars per month in 1902.[100] George died on June 10, 1904, and is buried at the Forestvale Cemetery in Helena, Montana.[101]

WHILE THE PHOTOGRAPHER OR studio was not identified on the back of the CDV, George Pew has made it clear that this image was meant to be a gift or calling card. He has signed the back "Respectfully yours," with his full name, rank and regiment. A previous collector has also noted in pencil that this image came from the album of the 137th New York's lieutenant colonel. Although the photographer remains a mystery, the studio provided George

Left: Lieutenant George Pew, 137th New York Infantry. *Right*: Back of Pew's image.

with a chair for his seated image, as well as a small, covered table to brace himself on. There is even a small railing behind him for decoration.

This image of George Pew gives an excellent example of the post–General Orders #108 sky-blue kersey wool trousers, with eighth-of-an-inch dark-blue piping running down the seam. His purchased dark-blue officer's frock can be recognized from the issued enlisted man's not only by its long skirting but also by its voluminous sleeves and short velvet collar.[102] Eight of his nine large buttons are visible; the ring around each suggests they are New York Military Shield buttons. These buttons have been left undone for comfort, besides the topmost, which has remained closed to comply with regulations.[103] Below his coat is what appears to be a sky-blue vest, with four small (possibly general service) buttons visible. Wearing a vest, Lieutenant Pew would be able to have his coat open in polite company if he chose to. Three small cuff buttons, likely matching the New York Military Shield buttons on his front, can also be seen on his left cuff. These, as opposed to his gold embroidered shoulder boards containing the single gold bar of a first lieutenant, were a subtle indication of an officer. George also wore a new paper collar or starched shirt, with a small black cravat. Most interesting, however, is the small white star on his left breast, the symbol of the 2nd Division, XII Corps, after March 21, 1863.[104] Between his rank, corps badge and the inscription on the back of the image, this CDV was likely taken in early 1864, prior to the tax on images being enacted. George Pew has his hair combed and his beard neatly trimmed for his image, but he appears worried, no doubt thinking of his loved ones at home.

THOUGH OUTNUMBERED, THE FEDERAL position at Culp's Hill held. On July 2, the fighting lasted into the night, with Confederate pressure picking up again on the morning of July 3. After the war, many of the soldiers remembered how crucial the breastworks (which General Greene had insisted be built) were to the defense of position. The soldiers profiled here served in four of the five regiments in General Greene's brigade. One of these men, Major Gilbert Elliott, paid the ultimate price and was killed in action at Lookout Mountain in the fall of 1863. Five of these soldiers lived into the twentieth century, while two of them died in the late nineteenth century. Each of these men carried the memory of the fighting at Culp's Hill with them, and after the war, the hill became a focal point for their monumentation.

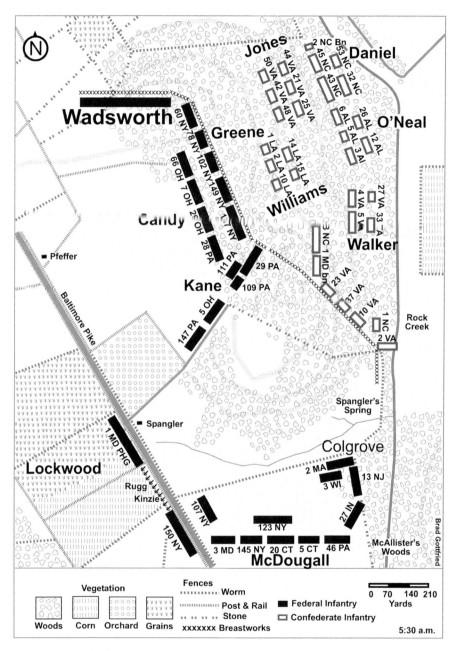

Culp's Hill remains in Union hands.

Chapter 2

COLONEL CHARLES CANDY'S BRIGADE

Colonel Charles Candy's 1st Brigade, of the 2nd Division, XII Corps, proudly led the XII Corps column as it approached Gettysburg, Pennsylvania, on July 1. Reaching the field near the end of the day, regiments from Candy's Brigade picketed the valley between Little Round Top and the Emmitsburg Road. Shortly after dawn, the XII Corps was ordered to the Federal right at Culp's Hill. There, Candy's regiments were placed in reserve behind the brigade of Brigadier General George S. Greene. From this support position, skirmishers were sent forward, and most of the day was spent constructing breastworks to help fortify the position. As the sounds of battle grew louder over the course of July 2, the majority of Brigadier General John Geary's 2nd Division was called on to move back south, leaving only one brigade at Culp's Hill. Thus Candy's men were moving again that evening, eventually deploying into line on the east bank of Rock Creek.[105]

Having been held in reserve for most of July 2, Colonel Charles Candy's brigade was ordered back to Culp's Hill around midnight, finally reaching its former position by 1:30 a.m. on July 3, 1863. Once more stationed roughly behind the brigade of Brigadier General Greene, Candy's six regiments were used throughout the fighting on July 3 to plug holes in the line or relieve those who needed to rest and resupply.[106] As can be seen on the map, the initial deployment of the brigade from roughly north to south was the 66th Ohio Infantry, on the brigade's left, with the 7th and 29th Ohio Infantry to its right and the 28th Pennsylvania Infantry on the right of the brigade line. Farther south were the 5th Ohio and 147th Pennsylvania Infantries. Slightly separated from the rest of the brigade, these regiments watched over what became known as the Pardee Field.

7TH OHIO INFANTRY

On May 24, 1861, the original three-month 7th Ohio Infantry was reorganized as a three-year regiment at Camp Dennison near Cincinnati, Ohio. Mustered into Federal service on June 20, the regiment shipped out late on June 26.[107] Unfortunately for the 7th Ohio, its baptism of fire did not go well. Attacked in its camp at Kessler's Cross Lanes on August 26, 1861, the regiment was routed. The following spring, the 7th Ohio took part in the 1862 Shenandoah Valley Campaign before being ordered to join the Army of Virginia under Major General John Pope that summer. On August 9, at the Battle of Cedar Mountain, the 7th Ohio was engaged in a fierce hand-to-hand struggle. Of the three hundred men engaged, only one hundred escaped the fighting unhurt.[108]

Transferred to the Army of the Potomac in September 1862, the 7th Ohio fought as part of Brigadier General George S. Greene's Division at Antietam. After the Maryland Campaign, the XII occupied Harpers Ferry and was guarding that depot during the Battle of Fredericksburg in December. The following spring, at the Battle of Chancellorsville, the 7th Ohio was actively involved in the fighting on May 2. The following morning, the 7th Ohio was relied on to cover the retreat of the rest of its brigade, earning the praise of Colonel Charles Candy.[109] Two months later, at the Battle of Gettysburg, the regiment was ordered to where reinforcements were needed most during the second day's fighting. By July 3, the 7th Ohio was back on Culp's Hill and dug in behind breastworks, from which it helped repulse the charge of the famed Stonewall Brigade.[110]

Following the movement west by the XII Corps, the regiment participated in the Battles of Lookout Mountain and Missionary Ridge and then pursued the Confederates to Ringgold, Georgia. Ordered to storm the heights, the gallant Colonel Creighton shouted to his regiment, "Boys, we are ordered to take that hill; I want to see you walk right up to it!" Caught in a converging fire, the charge was repulsed with fearful loss. The last service performed by the 7th Ohio was at the Battles of Rocky Face Ridge and Resaca, Georgia. After these, the regiment was ordered home to Cleveland. When the 7th Ohio mustered out on July 8, 1864, only 240 able-bodied men were present with their unsullied but battle-ridden colors.[111]

On July 6, Colonel William R. Creighton, commanding the 7th Ohio, wrote his official report of the Battle of Gettysburg. He wrote the following about the fighting on July 3:

My regiment remained at the intrenchments until near 8 o'clock, when it was relieved by the Sixtieth New York Volunteers. When relieved, I formed my regiment in the hollow at the rear of the breastworks, remaining until 9.30 a.m., when I was again ordered forward to relieve a regiment. I was not again relieved until 9.30 p.m., having been under fire of musketry most of the day.

About 11 a.m. July 3, I observed a white flag thrown out from the rocks in front of our intrenchments. I immediately ordered my men to cease firing, when 78 of the enemy advanced and surrendered, including 3 captains, 2 first lieutenants, and 2 second lieutenants. At the time the white flag was raised, a mounted rebel officer (Maj. Leigh, assistant adjutant-general to Gen. Ewell [Edward Johnson]), was seen to come forward and endeavor to stop the surrender, when he was fired upon by my men and instantly killed.

Colonel William R. Creighton

Commanding the 7th Ohio Infantry on that bloody hillside during the July 3 fighting was Colonel William Creighton. William was a transplant to the Buckeye State, having been born in June 1837 in Pittsburg, Pennsylvania. Before the war, he worked as a compositor or typesetter for the *Cleveland Herald* and was a lieutenant in the Cleveland Light Guard Zouaves, a militia company.[112] At the opening of hostilities, William first served in the three-month version of the 7th Ohio. Having raised a company himself, he was mustered in as captain of Company A on April 19, 1861. Amid his responsibilities, he married Eleanor Quirk on May 1, 1861. Five days later, the regiment was moved to Camp Dennison near Cincinnati, Ohio, and on May 7, William was elected the lieutenant colonel and drill master of the regiment due to his skills as an officer. He served in this capacity until June 19, when all the three-month 7th Ohio officers were reelected to serve in the three-year 7th Ohio Infantry.[113]

Sent east with the regiment in late June 1861, William is listed as on leave during the month of December. Returning to duty after the new year, he commanded the regiment in February 1862 and through its first combat at Kernstown, Virginia, on March 23, 1862. On May 20, William was promoted to colonel of the 7th Ohio and continued to command the regiment until August 9, 1862, when he was severely wounded at the Battle of Cedar Mountain. Described as a gunshot wound to the left side and arm, this resulted in William missing the Battle of Antietam. Following his initial recovery in Washington, he went on leave for twenty days starting on September 13, returning to Cleveland, Ohio. That winter, with the XII Corps in quarters near Dumfries,

Virginia, William commanded the brigade during the months of February and March 1863. Due to sickness in his family, he requested leave again on March 31. This was granted on April 4, and he was absent from April 7 to April 22. After this, he returned to command of the regiment and led the men through Chancellorsville that May and Gettysburg in July. In August, William and the 7th Ohio were briefly stationed in New York Harbor prior to being sent west with the rest of the XII Corps. On November 24–27, through the fighting at Lookout Mountain, Missionary Ridge and Ringgold Gap, William was again in command of the 1st Brigade, 2nd Division, XII Corps. Sadly, his time in command was cut short when he was killed in action on November 27, 1863, during the Battle of Ringgold Gap.[114] During the battle, he had ordered forward the 7th Ohio, then commanded by Lieutenant Colonel Crane, telling the men, "We are ordered to take those heights, and I expect to see you roosters walk right over them!" He then drew his sword and led the brigade forward. During the advance, Lieutenant Colonel Crane was cut down, and William, while attempting to recover Crane's body, was mortally wounded. Both officers were finally removed from the field, and William Creighton passed away six hours later.[115] Creighton and Crane were taken back to Cleveland, where their bodies were laid in state at city hall on December 7 and 8. On December 8, they were removed to a vault for the winter, escorted there by discharged members of the 7th Ohio, the local militia and a host of dignitaries, as well as the public.[116] The following summer, William Creighton was laid to rest in Section 14, Lot 43, Grave W ½; to this day, Orrin Crane rests next to him.[117]

As advertised on the back of the CDV, this image was taken at the studio of photographer James F. Ryder in Cleveland, Ohio. A three-quarter standing view of Colonel William Creighton, this image was likely produced during his leave of absence in either the fall of 1862 or in the early spring of 1863. William would have had ample opportunity in either case and was a full colonel by that point, as indicated by the embroidered eagle that can barely be made out on his right shoulder board. The boards, though washed out, appear to also have the extra-thick (or "extra rich") gold embroidery going around the edge and are an example of officers having to buy their own uniforms and paying a bit extra for upgrades.[118] William's frock coat is dark blue and double-breasted, with two rows of seven large federal eagle buttons running down the front.[119] Only six of the buttons are visible on his right side, however, due to his turned-out velvet lapels. His cuffs may also be velvet, and he has two small federal eagle buttons on his right cuff. William

Left: Colonel William Creighton, 7th Ohio Infantry. *Right*: Back of Creighton's image.

is wearing his frock open, likely for comfort, and a white shirt can be seen beneath. He wears a dark-blue set of trousers, a common occurrence with officers, and has a small black cravat around his neck. William's kepi, worn at a slightly jaunty angle, is particularly interesting, as it is a French chasseur-style kepi, with its stiff black visor and black piping on a dark-blue body. The crown has also been counter sunk, and the decorative knot can just barely be distinguished. It is the front of the kepi that draws the most attention, however, as William has used one-inch brass letters and numerals to spell out "7 Ohio."[120] As a final touch, William also trimmed his long mustache.

Lieutenant Colonel Orrin Crane

Commanding half the 7th Ohio Infantry during the confused fighting on Culp's Hill was Lieutenant Colonel Orrin J. Crane. Born in 1828 in Troy, New York, by 1861 Orrin was in Cleveland, Ohio, working as a carpenter for a Great Lakes ship manufacturer. When Fort Sumter was fired on that April, he enlisted in the Cleveland Light Guard Zouaves, which became Company A of the 7th Ohio.[121] Orrin was twenty-eight years old when he mustered into Company A of the 7th Ohio Volunteer Infantry as a first lieutenant on April 19, 1861. On June 13, 1861, Orrin was promoted to captain of his company. Just shy of a year later, on May 25, 1862, Orrin was again promoted, this time to major of the 7th Ohio. His final promotion, to lieutenant colonel, the rank he held at Gettysburg, took place on March 2, 1863.[122] Sadly, although he survived numerous engagements with the Army of the Potomac, Orrin's luck ran out following the XII Corp's transfer to the Western Theater. Orrin Crane was killed leading the 7th Ohio into action on November 27, 1863, at the Battle of Ringgold, Georgia. According to his pension card, Esther L. Crane, his wife and mother of Orrin's two children, filed for a pension on January 25, 1864.[123] Some of the details surrounding Orrin's death were described in the regimental history of the 7th Ohio:

> Crane was killed near the top of the ridge, and the men forced to retire. Creighton rallied the regiment and tried to reach the body of Crane, crying out that they must carry off the body, even if the charge failed; but it was impossible, the men had done all that men could do, and they were ordered to retire, which they did slowly and sullenly. While retiring the writer was shot and Creighton mortally wounded, and they were borne off the field together, Creighton dying within six hours thereafter.[124]

The remains of both Colonel Creighton and Lieutenant Colonel Crane were returned to Cleveland, Ohio, where they lay in state at city hall on December 7 and 8, 1863. They were temporarily placed in the Bradburn family vault at the Erie Street Cemetery for the winter. The following summer, on July 3, 1864, they were buried side by side at Woodland Cemetery, where a monument to the 7th Ohio was later placed.[125] The commanders of the 7th Ohio reside there to this day.[126] Lieutenant Colonel Orrin Crane can be found in Section 14, Lot 43 E ½.[127]

THIS IMAGE OF ORRIN Crane was taken by photographer Jason M. Greene in Cleveland, Ohio. While there is no back mark, a previous collector has written Orrin's name, apparently misspelled, and his regiment. The date of the image is difficult to determine, for although Orrin's rank is visible on his shoulder boards, it is impossible to determine if this is a gold or silver

Evin Crone 7th Ohio

Left: Major Orrin Crane, 7ᵗʰ Ohio Infantry. *Right*: Back of Crane's image.

oak leaf, the symbols for a major and lieutenant colonel, respectively.[128] In this image, he is wearing a dark-blue, double-breasted frock coat with two rows of seven large federal eagle buttons, three of which are visible. Orrin also has on a crisp, starched white shirt, the collar of which can be seen just over the frock's collar. His thick hair appears to have been brushed, while his heavy mustache has also been trimmed for the image.

28ᵀᴴ Pennsylvania Infantry

Raised from across the state, the 28ᵗʰ Pennsylvania Infantry was the third three-year regiment raised from Pennsylvania. The regiment mustered into Federal service for three years on June 28, 1861, under the command of its colonel, John W. Geary, who later commanded its division at Gettysburg. Initially, the 28ᵗʰ Pennsylvania had fifteen companies, as opposed to the traditional ten, and was broken into three battalions of five companies each. Two of these left Philadelphia, Pennsylvania, on July 27 for Harpers Ferry,

Virginia, while the men of the third battalion joined their comrades one month later. During this period, the regiment guarded the Potomac River from the mouth of the Monocacy River to Antietam Creek, a distance of twenty-four miles.[129] Though vigilant on guard mount, the 28th Pennsylvania was forbidden to cross the Potomac at this time due to its gray militia uniforms. The regiment had hoped to have its federal blues by that point, but they did not arrive until late December 1861, when the 28th Pennsylvania was at "Camp Goodman," named for its regimental surgeon, near Point of Rocks, Maryland.[130]

During the winter of 1861–62, there were several sharp skirmishes across the Potomac, and in March the 28th Pennsylvania, now properly uniformed, helped occupy Leesburg and Upperville, Virginia. The following May, the regiment was attached Major General Nathaniel Banks's division and took part in the Battle of Front Royal during the 1862 Valley Campaign.[131] On July 10, the 28th Pennsylvania was assigned to the 2nd Brigade, 1st Division, II Corps. Two days later, this command became part of the Army of Virginia under Major General John Pope. It was with this army that the regiment fought bravely at both Cedar Mountain and Second Bull Run.[132] Following the retreat of the Army of Virginia back to the defenses of Washington, the II Corps was merged with the Army of the Potomac and re-designated the XII Corps, with whom it fought under at Antietam. The XII Corps recaptured Harpers Ferry on September 22, 1862, and wintered at Aquia Creek, Virginia. In May 1863, the 28th Pennsylvania suffered significant loses during the Battle of Chancellorsville before returning to Aquia Creek. On June 13, the regiment was ordered north to its home state. At Gettysburg July 2–3, 1863, the 28th Pennsylvania helped hold the Union right flank at Culp's Hill, sustaining only limited casualties due in part to the earthworks there.[133]

The 28th Pennsylvania remained with the Army of the Potomac until September 1863, when the XII Corps was ordered to the Western Theater and joined the Army of the Cumberland. Working with the XI Corps, these commands took part in the Battle of Lookout Mountain and in the Battles of Missionary Ridge and Ringgold. The following year, the 28th Pennsylvania followed Major General William T. Sherman's command through the Atlanta Campaign and the March to the Sea, ending 1864 outside Savannah, Georgia. In 1865, it saw its final action during the Carolinas Campaign and mustered out on July 18, 1865, near Alexandria, Virginia.[134]

Due to the 28th Pennsylvania's losses in officers, the official report for the regiment at Gettysburg was written by Captain John Flynn:

Agreeably to orders received from brigade headquarters, on the morning of the 2d, the regiment was thrown to the front along the stream near the right of the line of battle, and remained in that position during the day, supporting the line of skirmishers of Gen. Greene's brigade. Some skirmishing with the enemy, in which men were lost to the command. Retired at dark with the brigade, and formed line about 1 mile in the rear. Remained in that position until 12.30 a.m. July 3, when the regiment moved forward to retake the position left the morning before. Took position in the breastworks, relieving the Twenty-ninth Ohio Volunteers. Were under heavy fire while there, and lost during the engagement 3 killed and 22 wounded and missing. Were relieved, and rested in rear of the brigade until nearly 4 p.m., when we were again ordered into the breastworks, and remained there until 10 p.m. Again relieved, and again ordered at 2 a.m. to relieve the Sixtieth and Seventy-eighth New York Volunteers, still remaining there. [135]

Surgeon Henry Ernest Goodman

Treating the wounded of the 28th Pennsylvania Infantry and many others at Gettysburg was Surgeon Henry Ernest Goodman. Henry was born on April 12, 1836, in Germantown, Pennsylvania.[136] He was one of six brothers, all of whom served during the war, and at twenty-five years old graduated from the University of Pennsylvania in 1859.[137] Enlisting in Philadelphia, Pennsylvania, at the outbreak of the war, Henry was commissioned as surgeon of the 28th Pennsylvania Infantry on July 23, 1861. His early service records list his status as "not stated" from June 28, 1861, to August 1861. Henry was then "present" starting in the September/October period. His status returned to "not stated" during the first six months of 1862, after which he was again "present." While the reason for that absence is not stated, his records for November/December 1862 show that Henry had been detached for service at Harpers Ferry per orders dated November 15. During the early spring of 1863, Henry had a ten-day leave beginning on March 6, and as of April 5, he was detached again and assigned to the XII Corps hospital. Henry remained with the corps hospital until August 3, 1863, when he was returned to his regiment.[138] At the Battle of Gettysburg, Henry was with the XII Corps hospital on the Bushman Farm and is listed today as one of the attending surgeons on the hospital monument.[139]

Henry went west with the 28th Pennsylvania, and on May 16, 1864, he transferred to the United States Volunteer Corps as an assistant surgeon.

Left: Surgeon Henry Goodman, 28th Pennsylvania Infantry. *Right*: Back of Goodman's image.

This may have been a mistake, as two days later, on May 18, Henry was promoted to surgeon.[140] He was twice brevetted during his service, to lieutenant colonel and colonel, both dated to March 13, 1865, and ended his service as the medical director of the Army of Georgia. Henry mustered out of the United States Volunteer Corps on November 3, 1865.[141]

After the war, Dr. Goodman returned to Philadelphia and developed an extraordinary career. By the time of his death, he was the surgeon emeritus for the Medico-Chirurgical Hospital and a founding member of the Orthopaedic Hospital, as well its surgeon-in-chief. He was the acting surgeon for the Wills Eye Hospital for twenty years and was at one point surgeon-general of Pennsylvania. Beyond the medical field, Henry was a member of the Union League, a fraternal veterans organization, and served repeatedly as his chapter's vice-president and director, as well as on multiple committees. Dr. Henry Goodman died suddenly at age fifty-nine on February 3, 1896, near Tioga Station in Philadelphia, Pennsylvania, after running to catch the train. He had been having heart trouble for years, and it was believed that the exertion to reach the train overwhelmed him. He was survived by his wife, Mary, as well as their stepchildren, and was buried at the Trinity Lutheran Church Cemetery in Mount Airy, Pennsylvania, on February 6.[142]

THIS BUST IMAGE OF Surgeon Henry Goodman was taken by photographer Frederic Gutekunst in Philadelphia, Pennsylvania, possibly during Henry's furlough in the winter of 1863–64. On the back, there is some damage to the upper edge of the image, suggesting that it may have been glued into an album at some point. The image also appears to have been signed "H. Ernest Goodman Surgeon 28th Pa. V. Vols.," indicating that this was likely used as a calling card for the doctor. In the image, Henry wears a double-breasted, dark-blue officer's frock, with a double row of seven federal eagle buttons, four of which are visible, marking him as part of the regimental command staff.[143] His shoulder boards, which can just barely be seen, would have had a black or dark-blue interior with gold oak leaves and a gold embroidered border.[144] They may also have had the letters "MS" on the interior for medical service. Finally, Henry Goodman looks directly at the camera with his beard trimmed and hair combed, thereby conforming to regulations regarding facial hair.[145]

Sergeant Arnold B. Spink

Keeping an eye on the men of the 28th Pennsylvania Infantry was Sergeant Arnold B. Spink, born on May 29, 1842, in York County, Pennsylvania.[146] Before the war, in 1860, Arnold was an apprentice carpenter living with his family in New Cumberland, Pennsylvania.[147] On July 4, 1861, in Philadelphia, he mustered into Company I of the 28th Pennsylvania as a private. Six months later, on January 1, 1862, Arnold was promoted to corporal. By March 14, 1863, he had been promoted to sergeant and, on September 1, to first sergeant.[148] His service records show that Arnold was detached to the field and staff of his regiment on December 26, 1863, shortly after he had reenlisted. His reenlistment form shows that Arnold had gray eyes, black hair, a light complexion and was five feet, eight and three-fourth inches tall. He had last been paid on October 31, 1863, having drawn $29.82 against his clothing allowance, and owed the government $8.82. During this same period, Arnold was transferred to the Western Theater with the rest of the 28th Pennsylvania and was later wounded on May 15, 1864, at Resaca, Georgia. The nature of his wound was not specified and may not have been that bad, as he did not report to the United States General Hospital at Camp Dennison, Ohio, until November 26, 1864, and was listed as "sick" at the time. During January/ February 1865, while he was absent, his pay was reduced by $14.94 for "transportation," although he was also due an additional $4.00 pay per month for his promotion to sergeant. Arnold returned to the 28th Pennsylvania in

March/April and received a final promotion to first lieutenant on April 23, 1865. Following the Grand Review on May 23, Arnold's service ended on July 18, 1865, in Washington, D.C. His muster-out form shows that he was last paid on April 30, 1865, and that he had been on special duty commanding Company D of the 28th Pennsylvania since July 3, 1865.[149]

After the war, Arnold Spink worked as a brakeman for the Northern Central Railroad in Pennsylvania and as a carpenter in the Trullinger & Company lumber mill in Harrisburg, Pennsylvania.[150] In 1867, he married Roberta Snell, and together they had five children, three of whom survived to adulthood.[151] The family moved to Steelton, Pennsylvania, where for thirty-eight years Arnold was employed by the Pennsylvania Steel Company. An active member of the Republican Party, he was appointed clerk in the office of the county recorder in 1912. Additionally, Arnold was a member of the Sergeant S.W. Lascomb Post No. 351 of the Grand Army of the Republic and the First Methodist Church of Steelton.[152] On August 7, 1912, Arnold Spink died in Steelton after a long battle with cancer. Revered by the borough, Albert was repeatedly referred to as "Captain Spink" in his obituaries, although he never officially obtained that rank. His remains were attended by both the GAR and the Sons of Union Veterans, and he was buried at Mount Olivet Cemetery, Section 18, Lot I, Grave 6 in York County, Pennsylvania.[153]

BASED OUT OF HARRISBURG, Pennsylvania, the photographers Burnite & Weldon provided both a decorative chair and a brace for this standing view of Arnold Spink. The limited photographer's advertisement, as well as the double-lined border, suggests that this is a mid-war image.[154] This aligns with Arnold's rank also, as he was a sergeant from March to September 1863. While Arnold's records are mute on how or why he was in Harrisburg, we do know where this image was sent, to Steelton, Pennsylvania, which is written in ink on the back of the image. Arnold likely had family there prior to moving there himself, as Steelton is only five miles from New Cumberland. A previous collector listed Arnold's name, regiment and final rank, as well as that he was wounded in action, while someone else has tried to erase a common misspelling of Arnold's name, "Spinck."

The base of the brace that is running up behind Arnold can just be seen peeking out from behind his shoes. The shoes themselves appear to be a high-grade civilian shoe, with the smooth side turned out and polished, unlike the usually blackened exteriors of the rough out Jefferson bootees or brogans.[155] Covering the top of Arnold's shoes are his sky-blue trousers, as dictated by

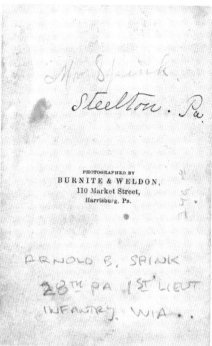

Left: Lieutenant Arnold Spink, 28th Pennsylvania Infantry. *Right*: Back of Spink's image.

General Orders #108, which established the color for Federal volunteers, along with the inch-and-a-half-wide dark-blue sergeant's stripe running up the seam.[156] At the waist line, a loop can been seen coming from underneath Arnold's dark-blue vest. This is likely a watch chain of some sort, while the vest is probably an enlisted man's vest allowing him to have his coat open in polite company. The vest itself is also open, most likely for ventilation, and has six buttons visible. Arnold's jacket is open, with the only the uppermost button and collar hooked. This made for more comfortable wearing while still conforming to the letter of regulations that the uppermost button be closed when out of quarters.[157] The jacket is a nine-button shell jacket, one of many variations that existed of this garment. Although it was officially discontinued by the United States Army in 1857, it continued with state forces through the Civil War. The buttons are quite large, and the top three appear to have a prominent ring design, implying that they are staff officers' buttons.[158] Arnold's position on the field and staff of the 28th Pennsylvania may also be the reason he has three cuff buttons on each wrist, a detail that is usually reserved for officers.[159] Arnold was not an officer at the time of this image, and his sergeant's chevrons are prominently displayed on both arms. He also has his corps badge, the five-pointed star of the XII Corps, on his left breast, as well as on his kepi. The star is white, indicating the 2nd Division of the XII Corps,[160] the famous "White Star" Division of Brigadier General John Geary. It is interesting to note that the kepi in Arnold's left hand is highly decorated with black braid and a Hungarian knot on top, as well as the previously mentioned corps badge slightly off center.[161] It seems likely that this kepi is, in fact, a prop provided by the studio as opposed to having been issued, although a private purchase kepi is also possible.

Arnold Spink appears to be deep in thought during his photo session. He stands clean-shaven, with his hair nicely combed and looking slightly down and away to the left. Perhaps he is thinking about family, the responsibilities of his rank or the challenges that lie ahead. In all likelihood, all these thoughts had crossed his mind.

5th Ohio Infantry

Though originally a three-month regiment, the 5th Ohio Infantry voted unanimously on June 20, 1861, to be mustered in as a three-year regiment. This was accepted by the government, and the regiment mustered in at Camp Dennison, Ohio, the same day. Ordered to the front on July 10, the 5th Ohio had a brief campaign in western Virginia trying unsuccessfully to intercept Confederate forces that had been routed at Corrick's Ford on July 13, 1861. The rest of 1861 was spent marching, drilling and scouting in western Virginia, as the men of the 5th Ohio learned the duties of a soldier.[162]

An active winter saw the 5th Ohio capture the Confederate camp at Blue's Gap and participate in the Affair at Bloomery Gap before settling into quarters in early March. On March 22, 1862, the 5th Ohio was ordered up and advanced through Winchester, Virginia. The next day, it reached Kernstown, Virginia, and participated in the battle there. At one point during the First Battle of Kernstown, as it looked like the Federal line was collapsing, Colonel Jeremiah Sullivan, the 5th Ohio's brigade commander, observing the regiment still fighting, exclaimed, "No, thank God, the brave 5th Ohio is still standing its ground, and holding the rebels."[163] Following the fighting at Kernstown, the 5th Ohio marched and countermarched through the Shenandoah Valley, eventually settling into camp during the last weeks of April 1862. On May 12, another series of exhausting marches began that eventually brought the 5th Ohio to the banks of the Shenandoah River by June 3. Five days later, on June 8, 1862, the Buckeyes took part in the

Battle of Port Republic, driving Confederate infantry from several positions and capturing a piece of artillery in the process. Immediately thereafter, the regiment repulsed a charge made on a Federal battery and was designated to cover the retreat when the battle was lost. In addition to its battle casualties, this rearguard saw 185 men from the 5th Ohio taken prisoner.[164]

The Federal defeat at Port Republic precipitated a lengthy retreat to Alexandria, Virginia, which was reached about July 1. There the soldiers of Brigadier General James Shields's Division, including the 5th Ohio, were given the opportunity to refit. By the end of July, Shields's Division was attached to the new Army of Virginia under Major General John Pope. The 5th Ohio served through the Northern Virginia Campaign, being bloodied at Cedar Mountain on August 9 and guarding the wagon trains during the Second Battle of Bull Run and Chantilly. Once the Army of Virginia retreated to Washington and was disbanded, the 5th Ohio became part of the Army of the Potomac in the XII Corps. Shortly thereafter, it stepped out on the Maryland Campaign.[165]

Although the 5th Ohio did not fight at South Mountain, at Antietam the regiment was in the division of Brigadier General George Sears Greene and fought to the top of Sharpsburg Ridge. From there, the men charged into the West Woods, holding the area of the Dunker Church for a time before Confederate counterattacks drove them out again.[166] Following the bloodletting at Antietam, the XII Corps was assigned to guard Harpers Ferry during the Loudoun and Fredericksburg Campaigns, thus sparing the 5th Ohio. On December 17, 1862, the regiment went into winter quarters near Dumfries, Virginia. Though attacked by Confederate cavalry on December 27, the regiment remained near Dumfries until April 26, 1863, when Major General Joseph Hooker's Chancellorsville Campaign began. The XII Corps helped stem the collapse of the XI Corps at Chancellorsville and retreated from the field on May 5.[167]

During the Gettysburg Campaign that followed, the 5th Ohio fought hard at Culp's Hill, particularly on July 3. After the transfer of the XI and XII Corps to the Western Theater in September 1863, the 5th Ohio had the honor of opening the Battle Above the Clouds on Lookout Mountain. The regiment then joined Major General William Sherman's campaign against Atlanta and reenlisted for the war that winter. After a furlough home, the 5th Ohio, by then part of the XX Corps, marched to the sea with Sherman and then north through the Carolinas Campaign. The regiment was present at the Battle of Bentonville and, following the surrender of General Joseph Johnston, joined in the Grand Review in Washington before mustering out on July 26, 1865.[168]

Colonel John H. Patrick, commanding the regiment at Gettysburg, wrote the official report for the 5th Ohio:

We commenced operations by an order to proceed to the extreme left of our line, and occupied a hill covered with trees. We deployed as skirmishers in our front across an open valley to a light strip of woods, and in front of that timber facing an open field, for the purpose of guarding against a flank movement of the enemy. We remained there until the following morning, when we received orders at 5 o'clock to return to the brigade. We advanced to the right of our line; halted, formed double column closed en masse, stacked arms, and remained until evening, when we were ordered to a position on our right flank, for the purpose of holding the enemy in check, for they had advanced on our right. We remained there about two hours, when we were ordered to return and take position. The men rested on their arms until daylight, when we were replaced, by an order from Col. Charles Candy, commanding brigade, farther forward, in order that we might have a better view of the enemy and be well protected from his fire. The first firing commenced about 3.50 a.m., and continued until 11 a.m. without intermission.

As the fight progressed and the forces took position, it became obvious to me that a line of skirmishers should be thrown forward on our flank and behind a stone wall, which would enable us to give the enemy a cross-fire. I immediately ordered Company F, of our regiment, in command of Lieut. Brinkman to advance with his company as skirmishers, having the stone wall for a protection. The result was most satisfactory, the skirmishers annoying the enemy so much that they were compelled to make a charge on our skirmishers, and either capture or drive them, neither of which was accomplished. As soon as they were fully uncovered, they received volley after volley, until they were forced to retire. The same effort was made a second time, and with the same result.

To the above strategy I attribute a large share of our success, for the rebels were driven back with terrific slaughter after the second repulse, and retreated from the breastworks. Very soon after this last repulse, we occupied the intrenchments. During the rest of that day and the night following, they annoyed us considerably with their sharpshooters. Some of them had air-rifles, and we could not discover their whereabouts. At night the flashes of the regular rifles can be seen, but there is no warning from the air-rifle. The enemy retreated from our front some time in the forepart of the night.[169]

First Sergeant Wilson B. Gaither

Watching over the men of Company D, 5th Ohio Infantry, was First Sergeant Wilson B. Gaither, the senior noncommissioned officer in the company. Wilson mustered into Company D as a sergeant on April 20, 1861, for three years of service at Camp Dennison, Ohio. While his 1861 records are incomplete, Wilson was first listed as "present" during the March/April 1862 period. This was short-lived, however, as he was captured on June 9, 1862, at Port Republic, Virginia, and reported as "Missing in Action." Paroled on September 7, 1862, Wilson was reported to be at Fort Delaware on Pea Patch Island, Delaware, on September 17. He was finally returned to the 5th Ohio on January 5, 1863. However, while at Fort Delaware, his records show that Wilson had incurred a debt and owed "John A. Hunt sutler $9.00 paroled POW at Ft. Delaware." Although these records do not show what Wilson spent the $9.00 on, he was due the "value of rations while POW June 9-Sept 7," according to his January/February 1863 records. There is also a note that he was furnished transportation from Baltimore, Maryland, to Washington amounting to $0.76. On May 1, 1863, Wilson was promoted to first sergeant and was noted to have received "transportation from Cincinnati to Baltimore," value unknown.

Wilson was listed as "present" for the next several months, including during the Gettysburg Campaign, but had his pay reduced by $0.63 for lost ordnance during November/December 1863 period. On January 4, 1864, Wilson reenlisted. His reenlistment form provided several details not originally noted in his service record. Wilson is listed as twenty-four years old and five-foot-seven, with blue eyes, a light complexion and dark hair. He also stated that he was working as a painter before the war. On January 11, 1864, his service records noted that Wilson had last been paid on October 31, 1863, and that he had drawn $60.22 against his clothing allowance and owed the government $11.22. In addition, Wilson's pay was stopped for a number of lost items, including a ball-screw worth $0.13, a spring-vice at $0.30 and a tumbler-punch at $0.20—these are all tools to assist in field repairs or maintenance of muskets. Interestingly, he was still due his "commutation of rations while prisoner of war, from June 9, 62 to Sept 7, 62." On April 4, 1864, he was promoted to the officers' ranks and made first lieutenant of Company C.

Money and payment issues continued to plague Wilson, as it was noted on his July/August 1864 form that he was due a seven-dollar-per-month difference in pay between the period he was a private and a sergeant. He was also due fifty dollars from his reenlistment bounty. On February 18, 1865, Wilson requested sick leave for an "enlarged Prostate Gland," and on March 20, the surgeon declared him "unfit for duty" while at the Officers Hospital in Beaufort, South Carolina. The treatment recommendation was for a thirty-day leave. Wilson returned to duty and was "present" for March/April 1865 with the note that he was due responsibility for money

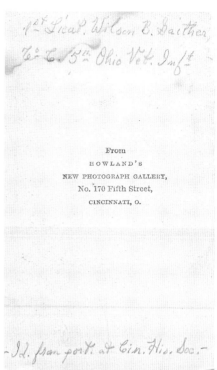

Left: Lieutenant Wilson Gaither, 5th Ohio Infantry. *Right*: Back of Gaither's image.

while in command of a detachment of the 7th Ohio that had been attached to the 5th Ohio from November 1, 1864, to April 30, 1865. On May 9, 1865, Lieutenant Gaither was promoted a final time to captain and was commanding Company B. On June 9, 1865, Wilson was arrested for being absent without leave and ordered to march at the rear of his company. He appeared before a court-martial on July 26, 1865, but there is no further information on the case. There is also no muster-out form in his records, just a note that on November 18, 1865, he was not under arrest.[170]

After the war, Wilson Gaither returned to Cincinnati and married Mary Cashman in 1866.[171] He returned to the painter's trade but sadly passed away just a few years later from typhoid fever on December 16, 1872. At the time of his death, Wilson was only thirty-three years old.[172] His pension card shows that Mary filed for a survivor's pension on June 12, 1889.[173] Wilson was buried at Cincinnati's Spring Grove Cemetery, Section 51, Lot 26, not far from the 5th Ohio Volunteer Infantry Memorial located in Spring Grove Cemetery.[174]

Pictured here in his first lieutenants uniform, Wilson Gaither had this bust image taken at the Howland's New Photograph Gallery in Cincinnati, Ohio. A previous collector has written Wilson's full name, rank, company and regiment, as well as noting that the image was identified from a portrait in the Cincinnati Historical Society. Though obviously taken some time after the beginning of 1864, due to Wilson's rank and the reference to the "5th Ohio Vet. Infantry" on the back of the image, it is hard to say exactly when this was taken. The lack of a tax or revenue stamp suggests that it was either before the August 1864 beginning of that tax or a copy of the original image purchased after August 1866 when the tax ended.[175]

Wilson wore his dark-blue officer's frock for this image, with three of the nine large federal eagle buttons visible. His shoulder boards, his symbols of rank, can both be seen, with the single gold bar of a first lieutenant visible on his left board.[176] Peeking above the short standing collar of Wilson's frock is a new paper collar for his shirt. Wilson Gaither is clean-shaven for the image but has combed and oiled his hair to look his very best.

Sergeant Mathias Schwab

On June 19, 1861, Mathias Schwab answered the call for volunteers and mustered into Company K of the 5th Ohio Volunteer Infantry. He joined as a private and stated that he was born in Cincinnati, Ohio. At the time, Mathias was twenty years old, five feet, seven and a half inches tall and of light complexion, with blue eyes and sandy hair. Before the war, he worked as an organ builder. As was common with early war records, his status was "not stated" until February 28, 1862. Mathias was "present" starting in March/April 1862 and listed as a corporal as of February 16, 1862. Just a few months later, Mathias was captured during the Battle of Port Republic on June 9, 1862. On September 7, 1862, he was paroled in Richmond, Virginia. Eight days later, on September 17, he was at Fort Delaware as a paroled prisoner of war. He remained there until January 5, 1863, when he returned to the 5th Ohio. Like his fellow parolees, Mathias was due pay for rations from June 9 to September 7, 1862. Upon his return to the regiment, he drew $25.74 against his clothing allowance. On January 28, 1863, Mathias was promoted to sergeant and was "present" until early November 1863, when he was provided transportation from Cincinnati to Louisville, Kentucky, on sick leave at a cost of $2.80. Sergeant Schwab reenlisted on January 4, 1864. At this point, his records become confused, as he had been assigned to recruiting duty as of March 1864 in Cincinnati, but he is also listed at/ in Dennison Hospital, part of Camp Dennison, for March/April. Mathias's health problems continued into the summer, for although he was promoted to first sergeant on June 13, 1864, he was sent to a hospital on August 28. This appears to have been his last hospital stay, however, as he was listed as "present" from September/October 1864 to his muster out. Shortly after his return to the regiment, Sergeant Schwab was promoted to quartermaster sergeant and transferred to the field and staff of the 5th Ohio on October 19, 1864. He was made an officer, a first lieutenant, on May 23, 1865. Another confusing aspect of Mathias's records is his muster-out date, which is listed as either May 22, 1865, or July 3, 1865. Regardless of the date, by the end of his enlistment Mathias had drawn $69.78 against his clothing allowance and was due $43.39 in payment from the government, plus $160 of his bounty.[177]

After the war, Mathias Schwab joined the Cincinnati Fire Department and by 1869 was the captain of Fire Company Ladder 1. Tragically, Captain Schwab died of burns and smoke inhalation on October 20, 1869, after leading an interior attack on the burning Merchants, Exchange and Mercantile Library.[178] He is buried in Block 7, Lot 3 of Saint John Cemetery in Saint Bernard, Ohio. The partially deteriorated inscription on his memorial states, "Captain Mathias Schwab of the…lost his life at the conflagration of the Merchants Exchange in the discharge of his duty as Capt'n of the… Ladder Fire Co. Oct. 20, 1869 in the 29th year of his age."[179]

TAKEN AT THE STUDIO of Campbell & Ecker in Louisville, Kentucky, this seated view of Mathias Schwab, seen here in his first lieutenant's uniform, was likely taken around the time the 5th Ohio mustered out of service in Louisville on July 26, 1865.[180] Other indicators include Mathias's rank, which he earned in 1865, as well as the card on which the CDV is pasted. These highly detailed advertisement backs were not developed until well into the war. Additionally, this gallery advertisement has included a box for a revenue stamp, which was only in use from August 1864 to August 1866.[181] While there is no indication that a stamp was ever on this card, it is possible that the tax was waived or, just as likely, that this is a copy of the original, which was sold after 1866. The Campbell & Ecker gallery specifically advertises that as an option.

Mathias's signature is on the front of the CDV, along with his regiment, indicating that this may have been a gift or calling card. The photographers placed him on a stuffed chair, with one arm propped on the tasseled armrest, giving the impression of a relaxed pose. The fact that both Mathias's frock coat and vest are open adds to this idea, as well as giving him some much-

Left: Sergeant Mathias Schawb, 5th Ohio Infantry. *Right*: Back of Schawb's image.

needed ventilation in a Kentucky summer. There is a significant amount of detail that can be seen in this image, including his dark-blue officer's trousers and the sky-blue piping for infantry seen running up his right thigh. There does not appear to be any skirting on this frock, indicating that it may be a field modified version of the formal coat. While seven of the nine large eagle buttons are visible, the lapels and collar have been turned down, covering the topmost buttons in a very non-regulation manner. The large sleeves and three small eagle cuff buttons of an officer's coat have been retained, however, as have his shoulder boards. The gold bar of a first lieutenant on a dark-blue or black field with gold embroidered border identifies the rank insignia as that of a staff officer.[182]

Beneath his frock is a dark-blue vest with perhaps as many as twelve small federal eagle buttons, although only nine or ten are visible. The vest being as open as it is exposes Mathias's shirt, possibly wool, with a very distinct paper collar attached. To keep with the relaxed theme of the image, Mathias has also decided against a cravat, although regulations called for it.[183] Finally, Mathias Schwab is clean-shaven and has a neatly combed head of hair.

66TH OHIO INFANTRY

The 66th Ohio Infantry was organized at Camp McArthur outside of Urbana, Ohio, in the fall of 1861. That December, 850 men mustered into the United States Army for three years of service. In January 1862, the regiment joined the forces of Brigadier General Frederick Lander on the Baltimore & Ohio Railroad in western Virginia. Their presence during the Romney Campaign helped convince Confederate forces to abandon Romney, Virginia. That spring, at Fredericksburg, Virginia, the 66th Ohio was brigaded with several other Ohio regiments under the command of Brigadier General Erastus B. Tyler, as part of the division of Brigadier General James Shields. It was within this command that the 66th Ohio acquitted itself well at its first significant engagement, the Battle of Port Republic. That summer, the 66th Ohio was ordered to join the command of Major General John Pope and fought at Cedar Mountain on August 9, 1862. Transferred to the Army of the Potomac as part of the XII Corps, the regiment was heavily engaged at Antietam but was fortunate to be in reserve during the Fredericksburg Campaign. At the end of the year, the 66th Ohio was part of the Dumfries, Virginia garrison that repelled an attack by Confederate cavalry.[184]

The following spring, during the Battle of Chancellorsville, the regiment held a position in front of Major General Joseph Hooker's headquarters. Later that summer at Gettysburg, the 66th Ohio helped hold the right of the Federal line, anchored at Culp's Hill. In the fall of 1863, the XII Corps was transferred to the Army of the Cumberland in the vicinity of Chattanooga, Tennessee, and was instrumental in helping to break the siege there. The 66th Ohio went on to participate in battles in Georgia that fall at Ringgold, Resaca, Kennesaw Mountain, Peachtree Creek and Atlanta. The 66th Ohio remained with the forces under Major General William T. Sherman through the March to the Sea, the Carolinas Campaign and the Grand Review before mustering out on July 13, 1865.[185]

At Gettysburg, the 66th Ohio was initially in support of Brigadier General George Greene's brigade, but due to a threat to the north end of the line, the regiment was moved forward. It crossed the entrenchments on Culp's Hill and moved to a position where the regiment could enfilade the attacking Confederates' right flank. This was described in the official report of the 66th Ohio, written by Lieutenant Colonel Eugene Powell:

> *I crossed with my regiment to the intrenchments in front of the First Corps, for the purpose of giving the enemy an enfilading fire. With my left resting on the intrenchments and the right down the hill, we poured in a murderous fire on the enemy's flank. After a short time I found that the enemy had posted*

sharpshooters at the foot of the hill, behind a fence, who were annoying us very much. I ordered my regiment to take up a sheltered position behind trees and stones, and direct their fire on the sharpshooters, whom we soon dislodged. I then received orders to recross the intrenchments and relieve the One hundred and fiftieth New York Regt., where we remained until relieved at 9 p.m.[186]

Captain John W. Watkins

Commanding Company E of the 66th Ohio on Culp's Hill was its newly promoted captain, John W. Watkins. John was born on February 23, 1838, and was twenty-three when he enlisted on October 19, 1861.[187] When the regiment was mustered into Federal service, John was commissioned a second lieutenant in the 66th Ohio. His service records show that he was present until June 9, 1862, when he was captured at the Battle of Port Republic. He was exchanged on September 21, 1862, at Aiken's Landing, Virginia, and thus missed Antietam. After spending some time at Camp Chase, Ohio, he returned to his regiment on October 21, 1862. Upon his return, John was placed in command of Company H and was present though February 1863, with a note in his records that he has been "cmd Co since Dec. 24, 62." On March 1, 1863, John was promoted to first lieutenant, at which point it was noted that he had last been paid on October 31, 1862. On May 22, 1863, Lieutenant Watkins requested a fifteen-day leave to visit Ohio. His leave was granted, but while he was away, he was promoted to captain on May 27 according to one record, while another shows the date of his promotion as June 27. Although John was present through Gettysburg and into the fall of 1863, he was listed as "sick" at Delaware, Ohio, in January 1864. He remained there until February and was back with the 66th Ohio on February 14, 1864. The March/April report for the regiment noted that he was "due for cmd Co. E $10 per month for Nov & Dec 63." On May 24, John was listed as sick since May 10 at Lookout Mountain, Tennessee. Due to this, he was sent to Nashville, Tennessee, to recuperate. When he returned to the 66th Ohio is not clear, but he was present by July 1864. On June 29, 1864, John was detailed as acting assistant inspector general of the brigade. He held that position until he mustered out on December 27, 1864, in Savannah, Georgia, having marched to the sea and completed his three-year enlistment.[188]

After the war, John Watkins married Nancy Tallman and was a prominent citizen of Delaware, Ohio. As such, he was a trustee of the Ohio Girls

FACES OF UNION SOLDIERS AT CULP'S HILL

Industrial School, the mission of which was "the reformation of exposed, helpless, evil disposed, and vicious girls." He remained a trustee of the penal school for nine years.[189] John did file for a pension on January 13, 1885, and Nancy applied for a survivor's pension after John passed. On the morning of September 21, 1899, John was not feeling well and chose to visit his physician. It was while at his doctor's office that morning that John W. Watkins dropped dead. Possibly due to an investigation, his body was placed in a vault and not buried until mid-October at Oak Grove Cemetery, Delaware, Ohio.[190]

THIS STANDING IMAGE OF John Watkins was likely taken while he was on sick leave in Delaware, Ohio, in January–February 1864. While there is no back mark or advertisement on the back of the image, it has been signed, possibly by John himself. Likely used as a calling card or gift, his name is given, as well as his regiment and a note that he commanded Company E.

Left: Captain John Watkins, 66th Ohio Infantry. *Right*: Back of Watkins's image.

The unnamed gallery has supplied a carpet on which to stand, as well as a chair and a brace. The ornate chair is a prop to rest his arm on, while the brace, the base of which can be seen behind John's legs, is running up behind him to keep his head as still as possible. Looking at the carpet, John is wearing a pair of black shoes, similar to an enlisted man's, but these are a higher quality, with the toes tapering a bit and the smooth side of the leather turned out for polishing. He is wearing dark-blue officer's trousers with an eighth-of-an-inch-wide sky-blue piping running up the seam.[191] John's frock coat is also that of an officer, with its very large skirting and voluminous sleeves being some of the more subtle indicators.[192] The frock has nine large federal eagle buttons, all of which are visible, and is hooked at the collar. Having unbuttoned six of the nine buttons, John is allowing for some ventilation and possibly utilizing a pocket, as many frocks had an internal breast pocket. Both of his shoulder boards can be seen, although the image has been washed out so that the captains' bars are not discernable within the gold embroidered border. Finally, he has a small white star, the symbol of the 2nd Division of the XII Corps, pinned to his chest.[193] While John has grown out a large mustache, he has kept it trimmed, along with his goatee and has combed his hair for the image.

THOUGH NO DOUBT EXHAUSTED after days of marching and countermarching, Candy's Brigade returned to Culp's Hill during the early morning hours of July 3. They were not allowed to rest for long, as Confederate infantry assaults began before dawn. Candy's arrival proved decisive however, as the Confederate attacks were repulsed, and those earthworks that had been previously abandoned were retaken.[194] Of Candy's men, the seven featured here all survived the intense fighting on Culp's Hill, although not all of them survived the war. Both Colonel William Creighton and Lieutenant Colonel Orrin Crane of the 7th Ohio had only a few months to live, as they were both killed at Ringgold Gap in November 1863. As for the rest, only Sergeant Arnold Spink of the 28th Pennsylvania made it into the twentieth century, with the rest of the men passing away in the decades following the war, most at relatively young ages. Although they had escaped Culp's Hill physically, the fighting there had no doubt left its mark on each of them.

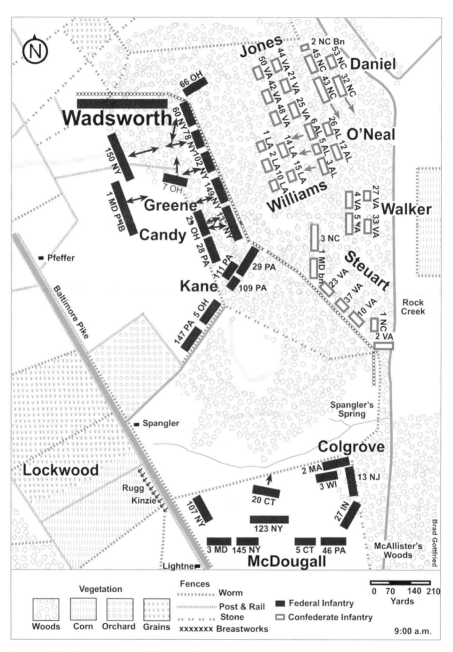

Colonel Silas Colgrove holds his ground.

Chapter 3

COLONEL SILAS COLGROVE'S BRIGADE

On the morning of July 2, the 3rd Brigade, 1st Division, XII Corps, went into position on the extreme right flank of the Army of the Potomac near McAllister's Woods and Spangler's Spring. Prior to reaching the right of the Federal line, Colonel Silas Colgrove assumed command of the brigade, as its usual commander, Brigadier General Thomas Ruger, was ordered to take command of the 1st Division. Colgrove referred to his position on the right as "three sides of an irregular square" and encouraged his men use the available stone walls or build breastworks for cover.[195]

Colgrove and his men did not stay in their newly built fortifications, however. In the late afternoon, on July 2, as the sounds of combat swelled to the south toward the Federal left, the XII Corps was ordered off Culp's Hill almost in its entirety. Among those troops moving south were the men of Colgrove's Brigade.[196] Although they raced toward the Federal center and left, these reinforcements saw little action, although they did receive some artillery fire. Finding the situation under control, the XII Corps divisions were ordered back to Culp's Hill and its immediate area. It was well after dark when they arrived near their old positions, and it soon became clear that part of their line had been occupied by Confederate troops. A hard fight awaited Colgrove's command in the morning.

Once again back on the right flank of the Union line, by 9:00 a.m. on July 3, Colonel Colgrove's Brigade, which numbered 1,792 officers and enlisted men in five regiments, was in a field just south of Spangler's Spring. Facing toward Spangler's Spring was the 2nd Massachusetts Infantry, while to its right was the 13th New Jersey Infantry. The 27th Indiana Infantry was to the right of the 13th New Jersey Infantry, while to the east in reserve along the Baltimore Pike was the 107th New York Infantry. In support of the brigade were four batteries of artillery, including Battery M, 1st New York Light Artillery. This battery was cut in half, with one section of cannons near Power's Hill and the other on McAllister's Hill. These regiments, though not the artillery, can be seen on the map.

2nd Massachusetts Volunteer Infantry

The 2nd Regiment Massachusetts Volunteer Infantry was one of the first three-year volunteer regiments authorized by the Federal government following the initial call for seventy-five thousand men. The regiment was quickly recruited in April 1861 and organized at Camp Andrew, named for the state's abolitionist governor, John Andrew, outside West Roxbury, Massachusetts. On May 25, 1861, the 2nd Massachusetts was mustered into Federal service. On July 8, the regiment left Massachusetts under orders to join Major General Robert Patterson, whom the regiment joined at Martinsburg, Virginia, four days later.[197]

Under General Patterson, the 2nd Massachusetts advanced to Harpers Ferry and garrisoned that place until August 1862. From there, the regiment marched to Hyattstown, Maryland, where it remained for two months, during which time the Potomac River and its fords were picketed and patrolled. Having moved to Frederick, Maryland, on December 4, the 2nd Massachusetts spent its first winter of the war near the city. In late February 1862, the 2nd Massachusetts advanced into the Shenandoah Valley and in early March was added to the division of Major General Nathanial Banks. Following General Banks's promotion to command of the V Corps, the 2nd Massachusetts became a part of Brigadier General Alpheus Williams's Division. On May 25, the regiment acted as the rear guard for Banks's command following the Union defeat at Winchester, Virginia. In early June, the regiment advanced again, passing through Martinsburg, Virginia, and Winchester and on to a position near Front Royal, Virginia, where it remained until July 6. Later that month, on July 17, the 2nd Massachusetts became part of the Major General John Pope's Army of Virginia. The regiment served under this command at the Battle of Cedar Mountain on August 9, 1862, where it sustained heavy losses.

Following the defeat the Second Bull Run, Pope's Army of Virginia fell back to the defenses of Washington. On September 2, 1862, Major

General George B. McClellan merged elements of the Washington garrison and the Army of Virginia into the Army of the Potomac. At that time, General Williams's Division, with the 2nd Massachusetts, became part of the XII Corps, Army of the Potomac. Advancing with the army, the 2nd Massachusetts fought at Antietam and afterward garrisoned Harpers Ferry before going into winter camp near Stafford Court House, Virginia. The following spring, the regiment participated in the Battle of Chancellorsville and in the Battle of Gettysburg that summer. In both battles, it suffered significant losses in officers and men.

In mid-August 1863, the 2nd Massachusetts was sent to New York City as a policing force following the draft riots in July. That fall, the XI and XII Corps were transferred to Stevenson, Alabama, and attached to the Army of the Cumberland. During this period, the 2nd Massachusetts guarded the Nashville & Chattanooga Railroad and chose to reenlist at the end of the year. The following spring, the Army of the Cumberland joined Major General William T. Sherman's Military Division of the Mississippi in his operations against Atlanta, the March to the Sea and the Carolinas Campaign. After this, the 2nd Massachusetts returned to Washington, marched in the Grand Review on May 24, 1865, acted as the city provost and mustered out on July 7, 1865, following four years of service.[198]

Lieutenant Colonel Charles F. Morse wrote the official report for the 2nd Massachusetts, describing his regiment's actions on July 3:

> *About 6 p.m. we left our position to go to the support of the left wing, which had been heavily engaged during the afternoon. We had hardly reached this place when we were ordered to return to the right. The regiment moved back by the left flank. It was ordered to occupy the breastworks on the left of the Third Wisconsin Regt. In order to do this it was necessary to cross an interval of open ground about 100 yards wide, over which the breastworks did not extend. Before moving farther forward, as it was then night, a few skirmishers were thrown out. A prisoner was captured almost at once. The regiment now crossed the open ground behind the skirmishers, and began to occupy the breastworks. I found that we were very near a force of the enemy, as talking could be plainly heard and a line indistinctly seen. Two men were sent to inquire who they were. They answered, "Twenty-third Virginia." One of these men was taken prisoner; the other escaped. The regiment now moved back across the open ground, and formed in line at right angles with the line of breastworks. During the night breastworks were constructed along our new line. At daylight, July 3, our skirmishers, Company E,*

became engaged. Firing was kept up until 5.30 o'clock, when the regiment was ordered to charge the woods in front of us. Col. Mudge gave the order, "Forward!" The men jumped over the breastworks with a cheer, and went forward on the double-quick. The fire while crossing the open ground was terrible, but the woods were reached and the regiment began firing, steadily advancing, and driving the enemy before it. I now took command of the regiment, Col. Mudge having been killed. I found on going to the right that the regiment that had advanced with us had never reached the woods, and that we had nothing on our right flank, and that the enemy were throwing a force in our rear. I ordered the regiment at once back far enough to uncover the right flank, which left the enemy in a very exposed position. They fell back rapidly, but lost heavily in so doing. I remained in my new position, inflicting a heavy loss upon the enemy, until my ammunition was nearly exhausted, when I sent to Col. Colgrove, commanding Third Brigade, for further instructions. He ordered me to bring the regiment back to the rear of its former position. The regiment after this was not actually engaged, although it occupied the breastworks on the left of the First Brigade during the following afternoon and night.[199]

Surgeon William Heath

The repulse of General Banks's forces near Winchester in the spring of 1862 left the 2nd Massachusetts without any medical personal, both the surgeon and assistant surgeon having fallen into Confederated hands when they opted to stay with the wounded. As such, the surgeon-general of Massachusetts called on Dr. William Heath to serve as the acting surgeon of the 2nd Massachusetts Volunteer Infantry that summer. Born on March 19, 1828, in Epsom, New Hampshire, William graduated as a doctor of medicine from Harvard in 1853 and the following year started a practice in Stoneham, Massachusetts.[200] Though recently married, he joined the regiment in early June and was convinced to take a commission as second assistant surgeon in the field and staff that July, formally mustering on August 5, 1862, as a first lieutenant. Not long thereafter, William was reported as "absent" sick in an Alexandria, Virginia hospital but was "present" again starting in September/October 1862. The following spring, on April 24, 1863, William was promoted to surgeon of the 2nd Massachusetts. He was "present" through the fighting of 1863, including Gettysburg, and transferred with the regiment to the Western Theater

J. W BARRETT,
Main St.
Stoneham, Mass.

William H. Heath
Surgeon, 2 MA Inf.

Left: Surgeon William Heath, 2nd Massachusetts Infantry. *Right*: Back of Heath's image.

that fall. He continued to serve the 2nd Massachusetts unit the July/August period of 1864, when he was detached to the Division Hospital. It was during this period that William contracted typhoid fever and died while on duty in Chattanooga, Tennessee, on August 28, 1864.[201]

William's service records contain a form with an inventory of his possessions at the time of his death: "1 Valise, 1 Haversack, 1 cap, 1 Jack coat, 1 over coat, 1 vest, 1 boots pair, 1 shoes pair, 1 socks pair, 1 gold pen, 1 sword belt, 1 looking glass, 1 cloths brush, 1 portfolio, 1 pocket book, 1 pocket cases, 1 Surgeon's Handbook, Money no cash, Money notes 50 dollars and 90 cents." They were turned over to J. Seeds, his nephew, who signed a receipt for the items.[202] His remains were returned to Massachusetts and buried at the Lindenwood Cemetery in Stoneham.[203] His wife of only three years, Delia M. Heath, filed for a pension on November 2, 1864.[204]

THIS SIMPLE BUST SHOT of Dr. William Heath is limited in detail but provides significant speculation. This CDV was taken in William's hometown of Stoneham, Massachusetts, according to the canceled tax stamps, on September 27. Although no year is provided, it had to have been between 1864 and 1866, when the tax stamps were utilized.[205] However, William had already passed by September 27, 1864. In addition, in the image, the two uppermost buttons on parallel rows can just be made out in this photo, suggesting a double-breasted frock coat, which would have been worn after William was made the regimental surgeon and thus a major in 1863.[206] There is also no evidence that William was able to visit home during this period. That, along with the slightly washed-out condition of the image, suggests that this is a copy of an earlier CDV, although when and where it was taken cannot be known.

Second Lieutenant Albert W. Mann

Among the men crossing the open, deadly ground near Spangler's Spring was Second Lieutenant Albert W. Mann. Born in Wrentham, Massachusetts, on August 14, 1836, Albert was a boot maker before the war. He had married in 1860, but at age twenty-four he enlisted in Boston, Massachusetts, on May 25, 1861, and mustered into Company E of the 2nd Massachusetts Infantry. Just a few months later, on July 14, 1861, Albert was promoted to first sergeant of his company.[207] Beginning in January 1862, he was listed as "present" for duty. That spring, on May 15, Albert was appointed sergeant major, the most senior noncommissioned officer in the regiment, and transferred to the field and staff of the 2nd Massachusetts. Almost one year later, on May 5, 1863, he was commissioned a second lieutenant in Company F at Stafford Court House, Virginia. Having fought through the summer of 1863, the 2nd Massachusetts was briefly posted to New York City before being ordered to the Western Theater that fall. Albert was soon ordered back east, however, to join a detachment in Boston on November 5, 1863, likely for recruiting purposes. Oddly, another note in his records dates this order from January 5, 1864. Regardless, Albert returned to the regiment in the spring of 1864 in time to muster out of the service. While most of the 2nd Massachusetts had reenlisted in December, Albert had not, and so he mustered out on May 23, 1864, in Chattanooga, Tennessee. He had last been paid on December 31, 1863. It was noted on his muster-out form that Albert was authorized five days' travel time to return to Boston.[208] Following the war, it appears that

Left: Second Lieutenant Albert Mann, 2nd Massachusetts Infantry. *Right*: Back of Mann's image.

Albert returned to the shoe business for a time but may have been working as a foreman when he died suddenly after a fire on August 28, 1881, in Saugus, Massachusetts, from heart disease.[209] Today, Albert Mann resides at Village Cemetery in Weymouth, Massachusetts.[210] His widow, Mary A. Mann, filed for a pension on June 5, 1886.[211]

WHILE THE BACK OF this seated image is blank, the front of the image has been signed "Lieut AW Mann." As this was taken when Albert Mann was the sergeant major of the 2nd Massachusetts, it's hard to determine if this signature is Mann presenting an older picture as a gift or if it is from another collector identifying Mann. In either case, the image was most likely taken in the fall of 1862 when the 2nd Massachusetts had fallen back into the defenses of Washington, giving Albert the opportunity to have it made. The unidentified studio has provided a high-back chair, as well as a small table on which to brace. Albert rests his left hand on a small book, the clasp of which suggests it is a photo album. For the picture, Albert wore his standard field uniform of sky-blue trousers, with a long dark-blue frock coat. Six of the nine large federal eagle buttons are visible, and the collar of the frock is clasped, thus keeping to regulations of being buttoned up when out of quarters.[212] On both sleeves of his frock can be seen large chevrons with an arch, the insignia of a sergeant major. The sky-blue color of the chevrons designates him as a sergeant major of infantry.[213] Another, more subtle, indication of rank is Albert's belt. This black leather belt is almost identical to that of a private, but the rectangular brass plate gives it away as a noncommissioned officers belt. This Model 1851 belt plate is more than two inches wide and bears the national coat of arms with a splayed eagle encircled with a wreath. The wreath was supposed to be silver and attached separately, but many variations of this plate were solid brass.[214] Finally, Albert has tried to comb his unruly hair and has trimmed his beard for the image, thereby keeping to regulations regarding facial hair.[215]

First Lieutenant John Andrews Fox

Part of the command staff of the 2nd Massachusetts Infantry, and right in the thick of its advance at Gettysburg, was First Lieutenant John A. Fox, the regimental adjutant. Born in Newburyport, Massachusetts, on December 23, 1835, as a young man John was in the first graduating class of Dorchester High School prior to studying civil engineering and working as an architect before the war.[216] He joined the regiment later than many, mustering into Company I of the 2nd Massachusetts on January 6, 1862, as a second lieutenant. His service records listed him as "present" from that point until February 1863. Prior to that, however, on August 10, 1862, he was promoted to first lieutenant and was transferred to Company F. On January 1, 1863, John was promoted again, this time to adjutant, the administrative assistant to the regimental commander, and transferred to the field and staff of the 2nd Massachusetts. He remained in this position for the remainder of his service, even declining promotion so as not to give it up.[217]

During the fighting around Culp's Hill on July 3, 1863, at Gettysburg, Adjutant Fox was present with his commander when the 2nd Massachusetts received orders to attack:

> *At about 7 o'clock, orders came to the Second, and one other regiment, to advance over the meadow, and carry the enemy's position. So strange an order excited astonishment. The regiments were a handful against the mass*

of enemy opposite, even without any regard to their formidable position.
Lieutenant Colonel [Charles R.] *Mudge questioned the messenger, "Are*
you sure that is the order?" "Yes." "Well," said he, "it is murder: but it's
the order. Up, men, over the works! Forward, double-quick!" [218]

Having survived the ill-conceived attack at Culp's Hill unscathed, John
Fox continued to operate as part of the 2nd Massachusetts command staff
when the regiment was ordered to the Western Theater that fall. Just after
the new year, John was sent back to Boston, Massachusetts, on an unspecified
detached duty. This proved to be a short assignment, however, as John was
back with the regiment by the March/April period. On August 8, 1864,
John requested permission to proceed to Bridgeport, Alabama, to turn over
the books and papers of the 2nd Massachusetts, as had been requested, to
the headquarters of Army of the Cumberland. Shortly after he returned, he
was detailed as post adjutant as of September 3, 1864. He remained there
through October but was back with the 2nd Massachusetts by the end of the
year and "present" until April 9, 1865, when he was absent on recruiting
duty. John returned and mustered out of the service on July 14, 1865, having
last been paid on April 30. Two years later, on July 16, 1867, John received
two brevet promotions to captain and major for "faithful and meritorious
services" as of March 13, 1865. [219]

After the war, John A. Fox joined the civil engineering firm of Garbett &
Wood before going out on his own as an architect. He briefly went south in
1871 to oversee the construction of the Tileston School in North Carolina
before returning to Massachusetts the following year. In 1878, he married
Josephine Clapp and was an active member in several organizations: the
Boston Society of Architects, the American Institute of Architects and the
Military Order of the Loyal Legion. Considered to be the father of "Stick
Style" architecture, he used this technique throughout New England. His
larger works in Massachusetts include the town hall in Provincetown, the
Home for Aged Couples in Roxbury and the Tewksbury State Hospital,
Male Asylum. Today, many of the Fox family papers are located at the
Massachusetts Historical Society. [220]

John filed for a pension on July 21, 1913, and passed away almost seven
years later on May 4, 1920, in Dorchester, Massachusetts. His burial at the
Forest Hills Cemetery and Crematory in Jamaica Plain, Massachusetts, was
attended by delegations from each of his social organizations. [221] After his
passing, Josephine filed for a survivor's pension on April 15, 1922. [222]

WHIPPLE,
96 Washington St.,
Boston.

John A. Fox
1st. Lt., Adjutant
2 MA Inf.

Left: First Lieutenant John Fox, 2nd Massachusetts Infantry. *Right*: Back of Fox's image.

This seated image of John Fox was likely taken shortly after his enlistment in January 1862 at the studio of John Adams Whipple in Boston, Massachusetts. For this relaxed photo, the studio provided a chair and decorative table for Fox to brace himself, while the table also acted as a hat stand. Although it is not possible to determine his footwear, John is wearing a pair of dark-blue officer's trousers, with the eighth-of-an-inch sky-blue piping, designating him an infantry officer, running along the seam of his right leg. Although these were the standard prior to the war, by December 1861, General Orders #108 had changed the trouser color of United States forces to sky blue, with the officers' piping for infantry being dark blue.[223]

While John is wearing some sort of dark-blue or black vest, a single button of which can be seen just above his right hand, it is his coat that dominates the image. An officer's sack coat or fatigue blouse, these simple garments were a mainstay among Union soldiers throughout the war. For officers, the sack coat was often cut large, acting almost as an overcoat, much like John is doing here with only the topmost button being fastened. Unlike the enlisted version, the officer's sack coat also has exterior pockets, the right pocket being visible in this image. The edges of these pockets, as well as the edges along the front, bottom and collar, are all picked out in black. In addition, the coat has three small general service eagle buttons on each sleeve and six large federal eagle buttons running down the front, five being visible.[224] Although his most obvious symbols of rank are slightly washed out, John's shoulder boards appear to be the bare rank insignia of a second lieutenant with a sky-blue interior for the infantry.[225]

Sitting on the table next to him is his officer's cap, a Model 1858 forage cap, also known as a "McDowell" due to it having been popularized by that officer. John's cap has the distinctive short, crescent-shaped leather bill, as well as a gold embroidered hunter's horn on a black felt patch sewn to the front of the cap. Within the loop of the horn, which is also a symbol of the infantry, a "2" is stitched in silver thread, for the 2nd Massachusetts Infantry.[226] Finally, John has combed his hair as well as trimmed his beard and mustache to look his best for his image.

27TH INDIANA INFANTRY

One of the earliest three-year regiments, the 27th Indiana Infantry was raised in late July and early August 1861, primarily from Indianapolis, Indiana, as well as the communities directly south and west of that city. The regiment was organized at Camp Morton, named for Governor Oliver P. Morton, on the Indiana State Fair Grounds, northeast of Indianapolis. Mustered in on September 12, the 27th Indiana left the state three days later for Washington, D.C., where it was transferred to Major General Nathanial Banks's Department of the Shenandoah in October.[227]

That winter, the 27th Indiana went into winter quarters near Frederick, Maryland. The following March 1862, it joined the movement in the Shenandoah Valley and occupied Winchester, Virginia, on March 9. The 27th Indiana fought at Winchester later that month, as well as at the Battle of Front Royal on May 23. Following the Federal defeat, Banks's command retreated back through Winchester, and the 27th Indiana was involved in the desperate rearguard action there for nearly four hours prior to falling back itself.[228] The regiment became part of Major General John Pope's Army of Virginia on June 26, 1862, and fought with that command at Cedar Mountain on August 9. Though not engaged at Second Bull Run or Chantilly, the Hoosiers were actively involved in the Maryland Campaign, having been incorporated into the XII Corps of the Army of the Potomac in early September.[229] It was the soldiers of the 27th Indiana who recovered a misplaced copy of General Robert E. Lee's Special Order #191, thereby confirming the separation of his Confederate Army of Northern Virginia in Maryland and giving further confidence to Major General George B. McClellan's pursuit during the days leading up to the Battle of Antietam, where the regiment lost heavily in the Cornfield.[230] Following the bloodletting along the Antietam, the XII Corps helped recapture Harpers Ferry, Virginia, acting as part of the garrison for some time. The 27th Indiana was fortunate to have missed the Battle of Fredericksburg that December and moved to the vicinity of Fairfax Station, Virginia, where it went into winter quarters. The following spring saw heavy fighting during the Battle of Chancellorsville and that summer at Gettysburg.

On August 16, 1863, the 27th Indiana was sent to New York City following the draft riots.[231] Though pleasant, its sojourn was brief, for in September, the XII Corps was transferred to the Western Theater and stationed at Tullahoma, Tennessee, during the fall and winter. A portion of the regiment reenlisted on January 24, 1864, and joined Major General William T. Sherman in Georgia. The 27th Indiana participated in the Atlanta Campaign, occupying the city after it fell in September 1864. Those in the regiment who had not reenlisted mustered out of the service on November 4, 1864. The rest of the regiment was transferred, first to the 70th Indiana Infantry and later the 33rd Indiana, with which the men served until mustering out at Louisville, Kentucky, on July 21, 1865.[232]

Lieutenant Colonel John R. Fesler wrote the after-action report of the 27th Indiana at Gettysburg just over a month after the battle, on August 8, 1863. Of the action on July 3, he wrote:

> *Just before arriving at the ground I had formerly occupied (or within 200 yards of there), I then, in accordance with your orders, sent one company forward as skirmishers, to ascertain if the position was unoccupied. The way being clear, I moved the regiment forward and occupied the ground, and remained there unmolested until between 5 and 6 o'clock on the morning of the 3d, and then received orders from you to occupy the breastworks erected by the Third Wisconsin on the night of the 2d. On arriving there, the enemy's sharpshooters immediately opened fire on the regiment from the breastworks built by the Third Brigade on the 2d. I was then ordered by you to charge their works. I immediately moved the regiment forward, but, on arriving within about 100 yards of their position, their fire was so deadly that I was compelled to fall back to the works I had previously occupied,*

which was done in good order. Remained there until about 8 a.m. on the morning of the 4th; kept up occasional firing on the 3d until about 4 p.m.; then, in accordance with your orders, made a reconnaissance to the right of Gettysburg. Found no enemy, and returned to position.[233]

Sergeant Peter Ragle Jr.

Advancing across Spangler's Meadow into the deadly fire near the base of Culp's Hill was Sergeant Peter Ragle Jr. of Company B, 27th Indiana Infantry. Peter was born on June 5, 1842, in Raglesville, Indiana, and was a farmer before the war.[234] He mustered into Company B on September 13, 1861, as a corporal. Upon enlistment, Peter gave his age as nineteen and was described in the Company Descriptive Book as five feet, nine and a half inches tall, with a fair complexion, blue eyes and light hair. As with many early war records, his status was "not stated" until March/ April 1862, when on either March 5 or 6 Peter was promoted to fourth sergeant of his company. Almost exactly one year later, he was promoted to third sergeant on March 10, 1863.[235] Following the near destruction of the 27th Indiana's color guard at Gettysburg, Peter was promoted to color sergeant later in 1863.[236] After the bloody years of 1862 and 1863, Peter was one of the few members of the 27th Indiana who chose to reenlist on January 23, 1864. Although the regiment did not receive a "veteran" designation, Peter was still allowed a thirty-day furlough home, as well as a $100 bounty.[237] The bounty proved particularly helpful, as he had last been paid on October 31, 1863, and owed the regimental quartermaster $12.23 for his clothing allowance.[238]

By the spring of 1864, the 27th Indiana had become part of Major General William T. Sherman's Military Division of the Mississippi. It was during the push through northern Georgia that Peter was badly wounded on May 15, 1864, at the Battle of Resaca. The casualty page in his records describes the wound as "severely in shoulder."[239] His wounding was further described in the regimental history of the 27th Indiana: "Color Sergt. Peter Ragle was wounded through the shoulder in the battle of Resaca, and Corporal Stephenson, of the Color Guard, was wounded by the same bullet."[240] As a result, Peter was sent to the Jefferson USA General Hospital in Indiana. He was later transferred to a hospital in Madison, Indiana. He received a furlough home to recuperate in September/October 1864 and rejoined the regiment just prior to the 27th Indiana mustering out of the service. With the

Left: Sergeant Peter Ragle, 27th Indiana Infantry. *Right*: Back of Ragle's image.

27th Indiana heading home, Peter was transferred to Company C of the 70th Indiana on November 4, 1864. Still troubled by his Resaca wound, Peter was back in a hospital by the new year and discharged for his wounds on May 5, 1865.[241] Wasting no time, he filed for a pension on May 30, 1865.[242] Later that year, Peter married Martha Trueblood on July 16, 1865, and together they had seven children. Martha sadly passed away in March 1879, and Peter remarried that September to Emma Gruver, with whom he had another six children.[243] Peter was also active in county politics and was twice elected as treasurer of Martin County, Indiana. He was narrowly defeated for auditor of the county in 1886 and seems to have left his treasurer post under a cloud, as the county treasury was found to be $7,000 short. While this debt was paid back, the legal wranglings over the missing funds, the payments and potential over payments continued for several years.[244] Following his time in politics, Peter Ragle spent his later years in real estate and passed away on December 19, 1918, in Elnora, Indiana, and is buried at the Raglesville Cemetery, in Raglesville, Indiana.[245]

THIS BUST VIEW OF Peter Ragle was taken by an unknown photographer and signed on the back with Peter's full name, rank and regiment. Likely taken early in his service, this image could have been used as a gift or calling card. For this image, Peter wore his fatigue blouse or sack coat, buttoned at the collar, with his vest poking out from his coat collar. Interestingly, he is also wearing a new paper collar for his shirt and a small cravat, an extra detail that was not required for enlisted men.[246] Looking slightly dramatic, Peter was photographed looking off into the distance; he has combed his hair back and has neatly trimmed his beard and mustache.

107TH NEW YORK INFANTRY

The 107th New York Infantry was the first regiment from New York organized following President Abraham Lincoln's call for an additional "300,000 more" in the summer of 1862.[247] The regiment was recruited from the counties of Chemung, Schuyler and Steuben. Rendezvousing at Elmira, New York, the men were mustered into United States service for three years on August 13, 1862.[248] The 107th New York left its home state in the early hours of August 14 and arrived in Washington to much fanfare the following day. Reviewed by President Lincoln and his cabinet, the New Yorkers received a new banner and were immediately ordered to the Virginia side of the Potomac River and stationed in the defenses of Washington for nearly one month.[249] When the Army of the Potomac marched forth from Washington at the beginning of the Maryland Campaign, the 107th New York was assigned to the XII Corps and was heavily engaged at Antietam. Following the nation's bloodiest day, the XII Corps helped retake Harpers Ferry and remained as part of its garrison through the Battle of Fredericksburg. The 107th New York did not see action again until the spring of 1863 at the Battle of Chancellorsville, where it again suffered heavy losses.[250]

In reserve at Gettysburg, the 107th New York was only lightly engaged and was part of the pursuit of Confederate forces back into Virginia.[251] In September, the XII Corps, along with the 107th New York, was ordered to Tennessee and was stationed along the railroad from Murfreesboro to Bridgeport. In the spring of 1864, the regiment joined in the movement on Atlanta and was heavily engaged in the fighting leading to the siege, where it was also involved. Following the Fall of Atlanta, the 107th New York moved out in November on Major General William T. Sherman's March to the Sea, as well as the final Carolinas Campaign and surrender of General

Joseph Johnston's Confederate forces on April 26, 1865. The 107th New York returned to Washington and marched in the Grand Review on May 24 before mustering out of the service on June 5, 1865.[252]

During the Battle of Gettysburg, the regiment was repeatedly moved, as Colonel Nirom M. Crane noted a lengthy report on the actions of the 107th New York during the battle:

About daybreak of the 2d ultimo, I moved with the brigade about 1 mile to the front on the pike, and took position, by your order, on the extreme right of the First Brigade.—Here we were ordered to build breastworks, or rifle-pits, forming a line in connection with the Second Division, Twelfth Corps,. About 7 p.m., the works being finished, I was ordered by you to move with the rest of the brigade to the pike. We moved thence and to the left and rear of the battle-field to the support of the left wing of the army, where a desperate fight was raging. I only remained in this position a short time, when we were ordered back to the old position of the day;—On our arrival near the wood (about 10 p.m. and quite dark), the Second Massachusetts leading, Lieut.-Col. Mudge sent forward a small squad of skirmishers to reconnoiter the ground, having been informed the enemy were or had been in the breastworks. Very soon after his skirmishers had advanced into the woods and reported the enemy in the woods in some considerable force.

The state of affairs was reported to you, and, after halting a few moments, I received orders to advance. The Second Massachusetts passed into the rifle-pits, and my regiment, by the flank, about 50 paces to their left and rear, into the woods. I halted when the battalion was about three-quarters its length into the bushes, and proceeded on foot forward to see the situation of the ground, &c. I had proceeded about 20 rods when I found myself very near a regiment of the enemy, who were in line some distance to the left, and in or near the breastworks. Not being discovered by them, I hastily retired, and meeting the acting major of the Second Massachusetts, he informed me that his regiment was retiring. I at once moved my battalion out of the woods across the swale, and reported the fact to you. I formed the regiment in double column, facing the woods, and let them lie down.—was ordered—to move my command to the rear of the First Brigade, form in double column, hold that position, and await further orders.

I did so, and remained until about daybreak July 3, when I received orders to report with the regiment near the wall, where found Gen. Ruger, and by his orders placed my regiment in the road to the left and in front of Capt. Best's battery, Fourth U.S. Artillery. Gen. Ruger ordered me forward a short distance to a crest of the ground, with orders to hold that position as long as possible. In this position we lay down, the musket-balls occasionally passing over and around the regiment. While here, the regiment was in considerable danger from premature bursting of the shells from our own batteries, which were firing over us, being some distance to the right and rear.—

About 4 p.m. I was ordered to the breastworks, to relieve the Forty-sixth Pennsylvania, which I did. While taking that position, the enemy's sharpshooters annoyed us considerably, but without injury. Near 6 p.m. I received orders from you to report to Col. Carman, Thirteenth New Jersey, for the purpose of proceeding about 3 or 4 miles to the rear with my regiment, the Thirteenth New Jersey, and Fifth Connecticut, to act as a sustaining force to Gen. Gregg, who was hard pressed by the enemy's cavalry. On our arrival near the scene of action, it was about dark, and the fighting had ceased; were ordered into camp until morning, expecting to renew the attack at an early hour. In the morning it was ascertained the enemy had disappeared.[253]

Second Lieutenant Edwin G. Fay

Helping guide the 107th New York during its movements at Gettysburg was Second Lieutenant Edwin G. Fay of Company C. Edwin was born in 1841 and stated that he was twenty-one years old when he enlisted as a private in Company C on July 16, 1862. Three days later, he was mustered into Federal service for three years as a sergeant. Edwin was described as five feet, five inches tall, with a light complexion, gray eyes and sandy hair. He had been working as a clerk prior to the war. The September/October report shows Edwin G. Fay as absent due to his being wounded at the Battle of Antietam. He had been sent to a hospital in Philadelphia, Pennsylvania. While recuperating, Edwin was promoted to sergeant major on January 1, 1863, and transferred to the field and staff of the regiment. He returned to the 107th New York sometime in the May/June period and was promoted again on May 3, 1863, to second lieutenant. Now an officer, he was ordered to Company C. The following February, it was noted that Edwin had been appointed aide-de-camp of the regiment as of December 25, 1863. Just a few weeks later, on January 14, 1864, Edwin was made acting commissary at Warton, Tennessee. That fall, on September 14, 1864, Edwin received a furlough home for twenty days.[254] Edwin was noted

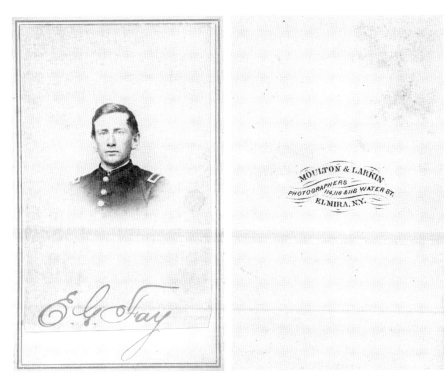

Left: Second Lieutenant Edwin Fay, 107th New York Infantry. *Right*: Back of Fay's image.

for his gallant service during the Atlanta Campaign, the March to the Sea and the Carolinas Campaign.[255] He served through to the end of the war and mustered out with the rest of the 107th New York on June 5, 1865, in Washington, having last been paid on January 31. After the war, Edwin was twice brevetted, to first lieutenant on October 14, 1865, and again on June 22, 1867, for "gallant and meritorious service as the Battle of Kinston N.C."—the second brevet was to captain for the same action and dates.[256] Married in 1868 to Sarah Young, Edwin moved to Philadelphia, Pennsylvania.[257] He resided there for the rest of his life and was a partner in a lumber company before retiring in 1876. Four years later, he won a lawsuit against his former partners after they used some of his stock to pay company debts.[258] During this period, he became a member of the Military Order of the Loyal Legion of the United States and visited Elmira to participate in reunions of the 107th New York, at one point even being elected to an officer's position on the reunion committee.[259] Edwin had filed for a pension on December 10, 1884, and his widow, Sarah Fay, filed for a survivor's pension after his passing; no date of that pension was given.[260] On June 12, 1902, Edwin Fay died in Philadelphia, and his body was returned to New York. During the funeral, his remains were tended to by the members of Baldwin Post No. 6 of the Grand Army of the Republic, prior to Edwin's burial at Woodlawn Cemetery in Elmira.[261]

THIS BUST VIEW OF Edwin Fay was taken in the Elmira, New York photography studio of Moulton & Larkin. It is likely that Edwin used this as a gift or calling card, as he has signed the front, "E.G. Fay." He is wearing his dark-blue officer's frock with three of the large New York Military Shield buttons showing—their prominent ring and bulbous design gives them away.[262] On his shoulders are his gold embroidered shoulder boards, the dark-blue interior with no other marking indicates that he was a staff officer with the rank of second lieutenant when this was taken. As such, this image was most likely taken when Edwin was home on furlough in September 1864. There is no indication, however, why the CDV lacks the revenue tax stamp that should be present, but it is possible that this is a copy made after 1866, when the tax stamps were no longer being issued. For the image, Edwin chose to look directly at the camera, revealing a new white paper or starched collar for his shirt, as well as a small cravat. He has also chosen to be clean-shaven and has combed his hair back in dramatic style.

Second Lieutenant Frank P. Frost

One of the more unlikely officers on the field at Gettysburg was Second Lieutenant Frank Frost. Having been three times rejected for service due to a supposedly weak physique, he was finally accepted on July 17, 1862, and enlisted as a private.[263] One week later, on July 24, Frank was mustered into Federal service in Elmira, New York. Joining the 107th New York, he was made the first sergeant of Company D. The Company Descriptive Book described Frank as twenty-one years old and five-foot-ten, with a light complexion, blue eyes and brown hair.[264] Frank was born in Millport, New York, and was raised in the Frost family following the death of his mother. As a young man, he had worked as a mule driver on the Chemung Canal, and before the war, he was a clerk in the Millport Post Office.[265] His service records show him "present" as of August 31, 1862. Something happened shortly after that date, however, as Frank was reduced to the ranks as of September 16, 1862, only to be restored to the rank of first sergeant by

Colonel Alexander Diven. He remained present for duty into the spring of 1863 and was promoted to second lieutenant on April 5 of that year. This may have been the formal promotion, as another entry in his records shows his promotion effective as of March 7 or March 13, 1863. Frank's records remained confused, as he is listed as "not stated" starting in October 1863 and continuing to September/October 1864. However, another form shows him commanding his company from January/February 1864 to August 1864. Another issue was Frank's promotion to first lieutenant on either July 9, 1863, or December 8, 1863—again the records are not clear.

Frank requested a thirty-day furlough on February 19, 1864, to visit his sick mother, but this request was "disapproved." He tried again on October 25, 1864, requesting a thirty-day furlough to address business issues. Again, the request was "disapproved." Shortly after this second attempt at a furlough, Frank was detached in November 1864 and ordered to 1st Division Headquarters of the XX Corps. He remained a member of the division headquarters until April 1865. Following the Grand Review in the capital, Frank mustered out with the rest of the 107th New York on June 5, 1865, near Washington. The last entry in his service records is a letter dated June 16, 1865, stating that "certified records [of the regiment were] lost on Hutchinson Island in Savannah River January 1865."[266]

Upon returning home, Frank married Rhoda Hutchings in 1865, and together they had three children. To provide for his family, he worked for the Erie & Pennsylvania Railroads at various stations until 1889. That year, he was made quartermaster for the Soldiers and Sailors Home in Bath, New York, a position he held until 1897, when he returned to the railroad. Frank finally retired, after forty-seven years in the industry, in 1920.[267] Throughout this period, Frank had an active social life. He was a member of the Military Order of the Loyal Legion of the United States, of Baldwin Post No. 6 of the Grand Army of the Republic (GAR), where he had been the adjutant since 1905. Along with many other social organizations, Frank was also a Mason and an active member of the Emmanuel Episcopal Church.[268] Among the many tasks that Frank was praised for in these organizations was his beautiful handwriting, with which he recorded the records of his GAR post and sent out memorial letters upon the passing of each member.[269] Seeing the ranks of his comrades dwindle, Frank filed for a pension on March 28, 1890.[270] He, however, did not pass away until November 3, 1934, at age ninety-three. He was buried with military honors in the mausoleum of Woodlawn Cemetery in Elmira, New York.[271]

Left: Sergeant Frank Frost, 107th New York Infantry. *Right*: Back of Frost's image.

According to his obituary, this bust image of Frank Frost was taken on the day he mustered out of the service, June 5, 1865, in Washington.[272] In actuality, it was probably taken a few days later as the Moulton & Larkin photography studio was in Elmira. The image was apparently meant as a gift or calling card, however, as Frank has signed the back, giving his rank and regiment in the process. The tax stamp has been struck out with a dated stamper, but unfortunately only the year, 1865, can be determined. In fact, this design of revenue stamp was not even meant for photographs. Besides a brief window in 1866 when they were authorized, this two-cent stamp is labeled specifically for "Playing Cards."[273]

For his mustering-out picture, Frank chose to wear what he would have had in the field. Instead of a fancier frock, he is wearing an officer's fatigue blouse. This is indicated by the turned-down collar and significant spacing between the buttons, only one of the five to six being visible here. Though washed out, Frank's first lieutenant rank can be partially seen on his right shoulder board as well. Appearing more relaxed in the field uniform, Frank has groomed himself for the photo, having trimmed his mustache and goatee, as well as combed his hair.

BATTERY M, 1ST NEW YORK LIGHT ARTILLERY

While the 1st New York Light Artillery was organized as a regiment, during the war most artillery regiments were broken up, with their companies or batteries being distributed to various brigades or divisions. This was the case for Battery M, 1st New York Light Artillery. Organized and initially commanded by Captain George W. Cothran, the battery, or group of cannons, was recruited primarily from Rochester, Albany and Lockport, New York. The cannoneers were mustered into service at Rochester on October 14, 1861, but did not leave the state until November. First sent to Washington, the battery was incorporated into the 1st New York Light Artillery and designated Company M. The command was then posted in the capital defenses and received six ten-pound Parrott rifles as its armament in January. These rifled artillery pieces fired ten-pound bolts. Now armed, the battery was ordered to Frederick, Maryland, with one section, or pair of guns, sent to Point of Rocks along the Potomac River.[274] The following spring, it served in the field as part of Brigadier General Alpheus Williams's Division, V Corps, then in the Department of the Shenandoah, through June 26, 1862. Transferred to the II Corps, Army of Virginia, the battery fought at Cedar Mountain but was fortunate to have missed Second Manassas. Transferred again in September, Battery M, 1st New York Light Artillery, was assigned to the XII Corps and was part of the garrison of Harpers Ferry after it was retaken.[275] The battery advanced south while the Battle of Fredericksburg was raging and wintered at Stafford Court House, Virginia, until April 1863. That spring, Battery M, 1st New York Light Artillery, was assigned to the Artillery Brigade of the XII Corps and performed gallantly at Chancellorsville, though with severe losses in both men and horses. These losses reduced the battery to four cannons when it fought at Gettysburg that July under the command of First Lieutenant Charles E. Winegar.[276]

That fall, Battery M, 1st New York Light Artillery, was moved to the Western Theater with the rest of the XII Corps. Eventually reaching Bridgeport, Alabama, the battery spent the winter of 1863–64 guarding the railroad bridge there. The battery was veteranized in February 1864 when enough of the men reenlisted. They received their furlough in March and returned to duty in April, bringing with them a number of new recruits.[277]

In May 1864, the XI and XII Corps were combined to form the XX Corps. At this time, Battery M received six bronze twelve-pounder smoothbore cannons, which it used throughout Major General William T. Sherman's Atlanta Campaign, the Savannah Campaign that followed and finally in the

Carolinas Campaign. It continued north to Washington and took part in the Grand Review on May 24, 1865, before mustering out of the service in Rochester, New York, on June 23, 1865.[278]

In support of the XII Corps at Culp's Hill was Battery M, 1st New York Light Artillery. The battery's locations are not on the map; however, the men did good work supporting the infantry, which was noted in the after-action report:

> *It was a small stone building about 200 yards from the creek on a nose of the hill that pushed into the floodplain opposite McAllister's Woods. These marksmen proved quite a problem for the Twelfth Corps troops who could not cross the creek and get at them. The men of the 13th New Jersey became especially irate when one of the snipers shot a stretcher-bearer who had gone to help a wounded man. Someone, probably Col. Ezra Carmann of the 13th New Jersey, sent for Lt. Charles Winegar, whose New York battery, had sections of Parrott rifles on both McAllister's Hill and Powers Hill. Winegar, came down and studied the site. He moved one of his guns from Powers Hill west across the pike to a place where it could get a good shot at the house. The gun fired a few shots and hit it. The Jerseymen cheered the lucky shots that drove the Rebels from the building.[279]*

Private Martin Schuck

Among the cannoneers trying to suppress Confederate sharpshooters near Culp's Hill was Martin Schuck, born in 1838 in Niagara County, New York.[280] Martin had mustered into Battery M, 1st New York Light Artillery, as a private on October 14, 1861. At that time, he stated that he was a twenty-three-year-old farmer but did not list a residence. His physical appearance was noted when he reenlisted in February 1864: hazel eyes, brown hair, a florid complexion and five feet, four and a half inches tall. In Martin's service records, the May/June 1862 report notes that he was "detailed on extra duty May 1." Martin's extra duties were expanded during the July/August period when he was listed as "Private on special duty as blacksmith since July 1/62." Martin was returned to his duties as a cannoneer prior to July 1863, as his service records show him as "present" for the period covering the Battle of Gettysburg. During the winter of 1864, Martin reenlisted on February 12, 1864. He had last been paid on October 31, 1863, and he owed the government $0.89 for a lost canteen and haversack. At some point in his service, possibly on May 3, 1862, Martin

Left: Private Martin Schuck, Battery M, 1st New York light Artillery. *Right*: Back of Schuck's image.

was given the job of artificer or handyman for the battery. He mustered out at Rochester, New York, on June 23, 1865, having last been paid on August 31, 1864. His clothing allowance shows that he had drawn $55.59 since February 6, 1864, and that he was still due $240 of his bounty.[281]

Martin returned to farming after the war and married Elizabeth Schuck shortly thereafter. The couple went on to have three children together.[282] Martin filed for a pension on March 19, 1880; following his passing, Elizabeth filed for a survivor's pension on October 4, 1915.[283] Martin Schuck died on September 18, 1915, in Wilson, New York.[284] He was later buried at the Chestnut Ridge Cemetery in Gasport, New York.[285]

LIKELY TAKEN WHEN HE was home on furlough in the late winter of 1864, this bust image of Martin Schuck was probably a gift or calling card, as he has signed the back with his full name and given it a little decorative flourish below the signature. While there is no additional period information on the back of the CDV, a previous collector has noted Martin's name and battery, as well as what collection the image came from.

Martin is looking contemplative in this image, no doubt wondering what the spring will bring for him and his comrades. He is wearing a dark-blue uniform jacket with red trim for the artillery.[286] The trim can be seen running down the front of the jacket opposite his buttons, as well as along the short collar of the jacket. Used almost exclusively for mounted troops, the uniform jacket utilized a dozen small eagle buttons down its front, as well as two more buttons on each side of the standing collar.[287] Martin has his jacket open, revealing a white shirt and civilian low-cut vest. He is also wearing a new paper collar and a large, dark bowtie. It is his hat, apparently a civilian hat of some sort, that draws the most attention. Martin has pinned what is likely a dark-red star to the front of the hat. This is likely a holdover from the Chancellorsville Campaign, when Battery M, 1st New York Light Artillery, was attached to the 1st Division of the XII Corps, the symbol of which was the red star.[288]

THESE MEN WERE AMONG those of the XII Corps who were shifted back and forth across the battlefield of Gettysburg on July 2 and 3. By July 3, they had been ordered back to their previous positions only to discover that the Confederates had moved into some of their breastworks. Due to this and the need to regain their lost works, Federal forces attacked, resulting in heavy fighting that morning in the area of Spangler's Spring. Of the soldiers profiled, six survived the war. In a sad irony, only Surgeon Heath died before the war's conclusion, taken by sickness in 1864. As for the other two members of the 2nd Massachusetts, Lieutenant Albert W. Mann died in the 1880s, while Lieutenant John A. Fox lived well into the twentieth century. Sergeant Peter Ragle of the 27th Indiana was wounded during the war, which resulted in his discharge from the service. He suffered the effects of his wound for the rest of his life before passing away in 1918. Both Lieutenants Fay and Frost of the 107th New York survived the war, although Fay was wounded in 1862, and they returned to civilian life. Fay lived until 1902 and Frost 1934. The final soldier, Private Martin Schuck, was an artilleryman and never reported being wounded. He lived into the twentieth century as well, passing away in 1915. Although they had marched and countermarched for much of the battle, these men and their comrades still found the strength to do their duty. Their return to the area of Culp's Hill aided in the recapturing the lost works, denying the Confederates their foothold and further securing the Federal right flank.

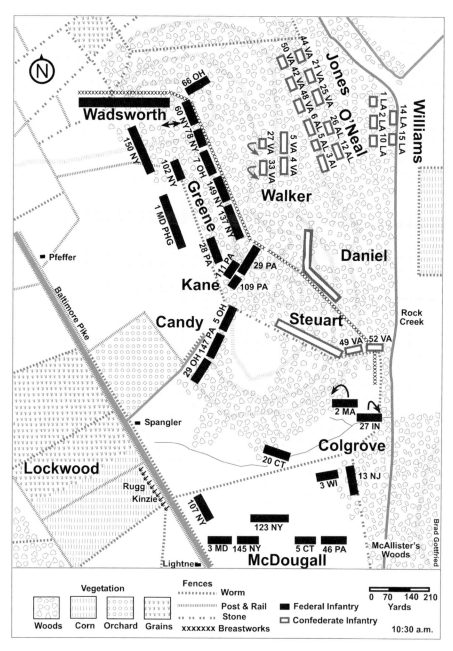

Colonel Archibald McDougall's Brigade holds the right end of the line.

Chapter 4

COLONEL ARCHIBALD L. MCDOUGALL'S BRIGADE

O f all the brigades of the XII Corps, the 1ˢᵗ Brigade of the 1ˢᵗ Division, commanded by Colonel Archibald L. McDougall, likely did the most marching during the Battle of Gettysburg. Like the rest of the XII Corps, McDougall's Brigade reached the battlefield on July 1 and did not participate in the first day's action. Up before dawn on July 2, the men were marched to the Federal right at Culp's Hill around 9:00 a.m. Once there, the brigade began to build breastworks, felling trees, stacking the limbs and piling rocks. By that evening, the soldiers of McDougall's Brigade were feeling very confident in their position.[289]

Unfortunately for the 1ˢᵗ Division, it was pulled off Culp's Hill that evening and marched two miles south to support the Federal left and center. The 1ˢᵗ Brigade was ordered into the Weikert Woods in line of battle, ready to advance, when word reached it that the Confederate threat had been repulsed and that the troops should return to Culp's Hill. This was done with some difficulty in the growing darkness, but the lead elements of the 1ˢᵗ Division were nearing their abandoned works by 10:00 p.m. At that point, as McDougall was deploying his brigade in the field south of Culp's Hill, it became clear that the breastworks were no longer abandoned. By midnight, it was determined that any effort to eject the Confederate interlopers would have to wait until morning.[290]

On July 3, the regiments of Colonel McDougall's Brigade entered the fighting on Culp's Hill with 1,835 officers and enlisted men. They were deployed south of Culp's Hill facing north with their left flank on the

Baltimore Pike. On the right end of the brigade was the 46th Pennsylvania Infantry with its flank roughly connecting with Colonel Colgrove's Brigade near McAllister's Woods. To the left of the 46th Pennsylvania was the 5th Connecticut Infantry. Slightly to the north and left of this line was the 123rd New York Infantry. Deployed in front of the brigade, toward the approaching Confederates, was the 20th Connecticut Infantry. Finally, anchoring the left end of the brigade next to the Baltimore Pike was the 3rd Maryland Infantry. This deployment, and the map, reflect the situation around 10:30 a.m. as the Confederate effort around Culp's Hill was ending.[291]

46TH PENNSYLVANIA INFANTRY

The 46th Pennsylvania Infantry was composed of men from the counties of Mifflin, Allegheny, Berks, Potter and Luzerne, as well as one from Northumberland. It was mustered into Federal service for three years at Harrisburg, Pennsylvania, on October 31, 1861, and was ordered to Harpers Ferry, Virginia, where it was assigned to Major General Nathaniel Banks's command.[292] Over its first winter of the war, the 46th Pennsylvania drilled, attended to camp duties and had the occasional skirmish along the Potomac River.

On February 24, 1862, Banks crossed the Potomac River at Harpers Ferry. As part of this advance, the 46th Pennsylvania moved south into the Shenandoah Valley and fought at the Battle of Winchester on May 25, 1862, during Banks's subsequent retreat. In mid-June, the 46th Pennsylvania was ordered to the Union Army of Virginia commanded by Major General John Pope. The regiment fought at the Battle of Cedar Mountain on August 9 but was guarding supply trains during the fighting at Second Manassas and Chantilly. Following the retreat of the Army of Virginia, the 46th Pennsylvania became part of the XII Corps and the Army of the Potomac. That fall, the regiment fought at Antietam and afterward helped recapture Harpers Ferry in late September 1862. The 46th Pennsylvania remained as part of the Harpers Ferry garrison for a time and was at Fairfax, Virginia, during the Battle of Fredericksburg. That December, the regiment had intended to go into winter quarters at Falmouth, Virginia. It was ordered out, however, in late January 1863 to participate in what was later called the "Mud March." The following spring, the 46th Pennsylvania fought at Chancellorsville and that summer at Gettysburg. It was part of the pursuit of Confederate forces back to Virginia and remained with the Army of the

Potomac until it reached the Rapidan River. Once there, both the XI and XII Corps were ordered west to join Major General William Rosecrans in Tennessee. The 46th Pennsylvania arrived in Nashville, Tennessee, and guarded the Nashville & Chattanooga Railroad between Bridgeport and Chattanooga for the rest of the year.[293]

In January 1864, enough of the 46th Pennsylvania reenlisted for it to be designated a veteran regiment. As part of the Army of the Cumberland, the 46th Pennsylvania fought through the Atlanta Campaign, the March to the Sea, the Siege of Savannah and the Carolinas Campaign. It returned to Washington in the spring of 1865, participated in the Grand Review on May 24, garrisoned the national capital through June and mustered out of service on July 16, 1865.[294]

The commander of the 46th Pennsylvania Infantry, Colonel James L. Selfridge, wrote the after-action report of the regiment's actions at Gettysburg:

> [P]*roceeded to a point in the vicinity of Gettysburg, Pa., arriving there on the evening of the 1st instant, and encamping for the night.*
>
> *On the 2d instant, marched to a position nearer the town and south of it, and to the right of the Gettysburg and Littlestown pike, and, by your orders, commenced making breastworks in great haste, which were completed in the afternoon of the same day, and I immediately guarded the same.*
>
> *At daybreak our artillery opened fire on the enemy, and several batteries in our rear, from an eminence, were obliged to throw their shot and shell immediately over my command, and from the premature explosions of our shells, and others from our batteries unexploded, falling in the midst of my command, I regret very much…*
>
> *During the day my command was much annoyed by sharpshooters, but I suffered no loss of life or injury in my command from the same.*[295]

Colonel James Selfridge

Commanding the 46th Pennsylvania Infantry at Gettysburg was Colonel James Selfridge. James was born in Berks County, Pennsylvania, on September 22, 1824. Raised in Allentown, Pennsylvania, James attended Lafayette College. Following graduation, he went into the mercantile business for the next thirteen years, first in Philadelphia and then in Bethlehem, Pennsylvania, until the outbreak of the war.[296] Then thirty-six years old, James was commissioned a captain in Company A of the 1st Pennsylvania

Infantry, a three-month regiment, on April 20, 1861. He mustered out on July 27, 1861, and on August 8 he was appointed lieutenant colonel of the 46th Pennsylvania Infantry. As was common early in the war, James's service records show his status as "not stated," but in this case, the period of unstated attendance extended through the January/February 1863 report. What is noted on his September/October 1862 report is that James was on special duty commanding the 128th Pennsylvania Infantry in September. During this period, he was also on a ten-day leave to obtain volunteers until October 27, 1862. On March 14, 1863, James left on a ten-day furlough to visit his family in Pennsylvania. That spring, May 10, 1863, James became colonel of the 46th Pennsylvania, the position he held at the Battle of Gettysburg. Starting with the July/August 1863 report is a note that "Has Thos Mooney a Pvt of Co C as servant pay to be deducted for same." This note is repeated on the following reports except for February 1864, when James was on a thirty-day leave. During this period, James was also absent starting in September 1863 through December on court-martial duty. In November, Colonel Selfridge assumed command of the brigade and remained its commander until his discharge. Mustering out on July 16, 1865, at Alexandria, Virginia, with the rest of the 46th Pennsylvania, James Selfridge had been breveted a brigadier general on March 13, 1865, for gallant service during the campaigns in Georgia and South Carolina.[297]

During the war, James was nominated for Congress in 1864 for the 11th District of Pennsylvania. Though defeated in that effort, he was made the assessor of internal revenue for the 11th District and took office in September 1865. In this role, he investigated the expenditures for the Antietam and Gettysburg National Cemeteries. He was commissioned a major general in the Pennsylvania National Guard in 1867 and that same year was nominated for the Pennsylvania State Senate. Defeated once again, he was elected in 1868 as the chief clerk of the Pennsylvania House of Representatives. In 1872, James became the owner of the LeHigh Cement Works at Siegfried's Bridge, Pennsylvania, where he resided until 1879. That year he was appointed health officer for Philadelphia, Pennsylvania, and remained so until replaced in 1884. When he left his accounts were shown to be short some $3,000. Although this was paid back, James's reputation was damaged.[298]

Following James's retirement in Philadelphia, his health began to fail, and he suffered for several years from Bright's disease. Due to the intensity of the disease, on May 19, 1887, James Selfridge fatally shot himself not far from his Philadelphia home.[299] He left behind his ailing wife, Emma, whom he had married in 1867, as well as four of his five children. He had been a longtime

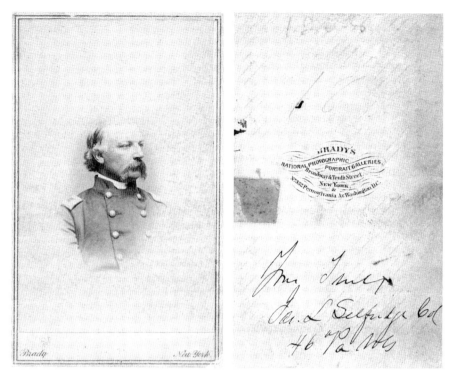

Left: Colonel James Selfridge, 46th Pennsylvania Infantry. *Right*: Back of Selfridge's image.

member of the Masons, the Washington Grays, Post No. 2 of the Grand Army of the Republic, and Philadelphia Lodge No. 73 of the Ancient Order of United Workmen at the time of his death.[300] He had filed for a pension on July 25, 1884, and Emma Selfridge later claimed a survivor's pension.[301] Buried in Bethlehem, Pennsylvania, at the Nisky Hill Cemetery, his grave is located at plot C 110.[302]

THIS IMAGE OF JAMES Selfridge, seen here in his lieutenant colonel's uniform, was likely taken at the beginning of his enlistment with the 46th Pennsylvania Infantry and was apparently a gift, as he has signed in "Yours Truly" with his full name, rank and regiment. This CDV was taken at Mathew Brady's famous National Photographic Portrait Gallery. While Brady had a gallery in Washington, this was taken at his New York gallery, as indicated on the front of the image.

In this image, Selfridge is wearing his dark-blue, double-breasted officer's frock coat. The dual row of seven large federal eagle buttons are plainly visible, although the "I" for infantry cannot be made out within the shield on the buttons.[303] James shoulder boards are also visible, and the gold embroidered borders appear to be thicker that the standard quarter inch and are likely "extra rich" where the officer has paid for more embroidery. The actual symbol of rank within the embroidered border is a silver oak leaf at each end signifying a lieutenant colonel.[304] It is interesting to note that while James is wearing either a new paper collar or a freshly starched shirt, he is missing his cravat, which was also a requirement for officers' uniforms at the time. He has, however, neatly combed his thinning hair and trimmed his mustache.[305]

5th Connecticut Infantry

The men who made up the 5th Connecticut Infantry had originally been organized as Colt's First Regiment of Revolving Rifles under the command of Samuel Colt of the Colt Patent Fire Arms Company. Before that, many of those same men had enlisted for three months after the initial call for seventy-five thousand volunteers in April 1861. The Colt Revolving Rifle Regiment was disbanded on June 20, 1861; that same day, the men reenlisted into the 5th Connecticut Volunteer Infantry, commanded by Colonel Orris S. Ferry. Two days later, the regiment marched to Camp Putnam, where it was equipped for service and continued to drill. There, one month later, on July 22–23, the 5th Connecticut was mustered into the service of the United States.[306]

The 5th Connecticut left the state on July 29 and arrived at Sandy Hook, Maryland, two days later. While stationed at Sandy Hook, the regiment's primary duty was picketing and guarding the Potomac River. Ordered to Muddy Branch on October 26, the men went into camp until December. Throughout December, the regiment maneuvered on the Maryland side of the Potomac River, while Confederates under Major General Thomas J. Jackson threatened various points from the Virginia side. By early January 1862, both sides had settled into winter quarters.[307]

On March 1, 1862, the 5th Connecticut broke camp, and by March 3, it was over the Potomac River as a part of Major General Nathaniel Banks's command. As a portion of the vanguard, the regiment entered Winchester, Virginia, on March 12. Ordered back to Washington on March 22, it returned to Winchester the next day due to fighting south of the city. By March 24, the regiment was in pursuit of Confederate forces. Two months later, however, on May 24, 1862, it was falling back to Winchester.[308]

The 5th Connecticut saw its first large engagement at Winchester on May 25, 1862; although Federal forces were defeated, the regiment fought well. Having fallen back into Maryland, by June 3 the regiment was once more in the Shenandoah Valley, where it maneuvered against and skirmished with Confederate troops until early July. On July 7, the 5th Connecticut was ordered to Warrenton, Virginia, where it joined Major General John Pope's Army of Virginia. The Connecticut men fought at Cedar Mountain on August 9, 1862, but saw only limited action for the rest of August. Following Pope's defeat at Second Bull Run, they retreated into the defenses of Washington at the beginning of September. Attached to the XII Corps, the 5th Connecticut advanced to Frederick, Maryland, with the Army of the Potomac but was then detached to act as the provost guard of the city. There the troops remained until December 10, 1862, when the regiment marched to rejoin the army near Fredericksburg, Virginia, and went into winter quarters at Stafford Court House, Virginia.[309]

During the spring and summer of 1863, the 5th Connecticut saw active service during both the Chancellorsville and Gettysburg Campaigns. In each case, the regiment was detailed to build earthworks and, in each battle, had its works occupied for a time by Confederate forces when the regiment had been ordered elsewhere.[310] Following Gettysburg, the troops participated in the pursuit of Confederate forces back into Virginia and were ordered west with the rest of the XII Corps on September 25, 1863, to join the Army of the Cumberland. The regiment guarded the Nashville & Chattanooga Railroad for the rest of 1863. That December, 280 men reenlisted and received their veterans' furlough and bounty.[311]

Just prior to the opening of the spring campaign in 1864, the old XI and XII Corps were merged, forming the XX Corps. The 5th Connecticut fought with this command through the remainder of the war as part of the Army of the Cumberland. Heavily engaged throughout the Atlanta Campaign, the regiment saw the fall of Atlanta, Georgia, and took part in the March to the Sea, the Siege of Savannah and the Carolinas Campaign from 1864 to 1865. Upon returning to Washington, the 5th Connecticut marched in the Grand Review on May 24 as a part of Major General William T. Sherman's forces and mustered out of the service on July 19, 1865, in Alexandria, Virginia.[312]

Colonel Warren W. Packer commanded the 5th Connecticut Infantry at Gettysburg and described his regiment's actions in his report:

> *The following morning, July 1, marched from thence to within 1 mile of Gettysburg, Pa. We then filed to the right, and, after marching nearly 1*

mile, formed line of battle; were then ordered to support a section of Battery M, First New York Artillery. Upon being relieved of this duty, we were thrown forward as skirmishers.

On the morning of the 2d, we rejoined the brigade, which moved forward, taking a new position, which we proceeded to fortify by throwing up breastworks.

On the evening of the 2d, we moved to the left about 2 miles, remaining but a short time. Upon attempting to return to the breastworks, we found them occupied by the enemy, in consequence of which, after detailing Company E as skirmishers, they losing 5 men taken prisoners, we remained in the field until the morning of the 3d, occupying the same position until 12 m., when the regiment moved a short distance to the rear, taking position in a ravine, for the purpose of watching the movements of the enemy upon our right flank.[313]

Private John Alexander

One of the 5th Connecticut men likely involved with the breastwork building on July 2, 1863, was Private John Alexander of Company B. Almost two years previously, John had mustered into the 5th Connecticut Infantry on July 22, 1861. Born in Enfield, Connecticut, John was working as a shoemaker before the war. The Company Descriptive Book stated he was eighteen and five-foot-six, with brown hair, brown eyes and a dark complexion. In his service records, his initial status was "not stated," as was common in the early war records. However, the September/October 1861 report has a note that John owed the sutler $2.00, for what though was not specified. His troubles with money continued through 1861 and into the new year, as John had his pay reduced during the November/December period for an unstated infraction. On his January/February report, it stated that he was fined $7.00 by a court-martial; the charge, however, again was not listed. Starting in March/April 1862, John was "present" until the summer of 1862, when his July/August reported noted that he was a "nurse left in hospital Culpepper 5/62." The following reporting period mentioned that he had been "exchanged returned to the Regt." From that point, John continued to be "present" until January 11, 1864, when he was transferred to Company G of the 20th Connecticut Infantry. He remained with the 20th Connecticut for just over three months when on March 29, 1864, he returned to Company B of the 5th Connecticut. However, his pay was deducted $0.20 for ordnance

Left: Private John Alexander, 5th Connecticut Infantry. *Right*: Back of Alexander's image.

and ordnance stores. This stoppage was noted on the next report also, with a note that the missing items were "lost." Private John Alexander mustered out on July 22, 1864, after his three years of service. He had last been paid on October 31, 1863, and had drawn $29.48 of his clothing allowance since August 1. John was also due $100 bounty, but he owed the government $0.23 for a lost screwdriver.[314] Although he had served with both the 5th and 20th Connecticut during his enlistment, John's service was not yet over. In September 1864, he enlisted in the 202nd Pennsylvania Infantry and served until August 1865 as part of the Department of Washington.[315]

There is very little information on John Alexander's postwar life. Although no date of death has been found, his comrades in the 5th Connecticut mourned his passing on August 9, 1887, at the dedication of the regiment's monument near Culp's Hill at Gettysburg.[316] The only problem was that John was not dead. He is listed on the 1890 United States Census of Civil War veterans and widows for Pennsylvania and filed for a pension on February 18, 1891.[317] John did marry at some point, but his final resting place remains unknown.

As NOTED BY THE simple advertisement on the back of the image, this standing image was taken by photographic artist Oliver B. Buel at his Great Barrington, Massachusetts gallery. The gallery provided a chair to act as a brace for John, doubling as a display table for his dress hat. Additionally, a large decorative drape dominates the right side of the CDV, no doubt helping to obscure the brace that was likely placed behind John to help keep his head as steady as possible. No additional information has been provided on the front or back, but a previous collector has noted John's name, place of enlistment and his regiment.

While the limited advertising on the back of the CDV, as well as the lack of a border on the front, suggests an early war image, it is John's uniform that really gives it away.[318]

Likely taken in the summer of 1861 at the beginning of his enlistment, this image shows John in what appears to be a Regular Army uniform. This makes sense, as Colonel Samuel Colt had tried to have his regiment mustered into the Regular Army at the beginning of the war, and it was not until December 1861, with General Orders #108, that different colors were assigned to the volunteer forces.[319] John is wearing a pair of simple leather shoes, known as Jefferson bootees or brogans, the bulk of which are hidden by his dark-blue wool trousers. Coming to his mid-thighs is the skirting for his dark-blue frock coat. As with all enlisted men's frocks, it has a single row of nine evenly spaced buttons running down the front. The buttons are large federal eagle buttons, better known as general service buttons. There are two small eagle buttons on the cuffs of the sleeves as well, the left two being visible.[320] Over the course of the war, there were many variations of the frock. While this coat does have the sky-blue cuff and collar piping to signify infantry, it also has a tall collar, apparently lacking the regulation hook, as opposed to the short standing collars seen later in the war.[321]

Although he stands bareheaded, as previously stated, John's Model 1858 dress hat, also known as a Hardee hat, sits on the chair next to him. This was the headgear of the Regular Army at the opening of the war and was made of black felt with a three-inch brim. In this case, the right side of the brim has been pinned up, likely by a brass eagle, while the front of the crown bares a brass hunter's horn, the symbol of the infantry. Additionally, a sky-blue tasseled hat cord encircles the crown of the hat, while a single black ostrich plume can be seen sticking out of the cord.[322]

Sergeant Michael Donovan

No doubt keeping an eye on the 5th Connecticut's earthwork building efforts on July 2, 1863, was Sergeant Michael Donovan of Company D. Born in Salem, Massachusetts, Michael was a twenty-three-year-old currier when he enlisted at Hartford, Connecticut, and mustered as a private into the 5th Connecticut Infantry for three years of service on July 22, 1861. The Company Descriptive Book described Michael as five feet, eight inches tall with a florid complexion, gray eyes and brown hair. His service records list him as "present" through his entire service. The first note in his records states that on October 21, 1861, three months after joining the regiment, he was promoted to corporal. He was promoted again on December 9, 1862, to sergeant, just before the Battle of Fredericksburg. During the same period Michael fought at Gettysburg, his records for July/August 1863 misspelled his name as "Mikeal." Typos aside, his next promotion was to second lieutenant on either September 12 or October 13, 1863, as both dates are mentioned in his records. That December, Michael chose to reenlist and the following January 1864 was on "detached service," but there is no further information as to what that entailed. Six months later, Michael was appointed "acting Adj[utant] since July 20 64." His final promotion came on December 15, 1864, when Michael was promoted to captain and transferred to Company I. He remained with Company I for the rest of his service and mustered out on July 19, 1865, having last been paid on April 30, 1865.[323]

After the war, Michael moved west and appears to have been a tanner in California.[324] He never married and filed for a pension on October 10, 1893.[325] Two years later, he was admitted to the Pacific Branch of the National Home for Disabled Volunteer Soldiers in Sawtelle, California, where he remained for thirty-four years before passing away on January 17, 1929, from myocarditis, likely brought on by influenza.[326] Four days later, Michael Donovan was laid to rest at Los Angeles National Cemetery, plot 59, 4 R G.[327]

THIS BUST IMAGE OF Michael Donovan was taken at the Snell Studio in Salem, Massachusetts, in his second lieutenant's uniform. Michael likely used this image as a calling card, as he has signed the back, as well as gave his rank, regiment and home address. A previous collector also wrote his name in pencil on the back. Additionally, it should be noted that Michael's rank for his signature does not match the image. This CDV was given away

Left: Sergeant Michael Donovan, 5th Connecticut Infantry. *Right*: Back of Donovan's image.

after December 1864, when Michael was made captain of Company I, but the image itself had been taken after he was made a second lieutenant in the fall of 1863. The lack of a revenue stamp also suggests that this image was made prior to August 1864, when the tax stamps started being used.[328]

Though only a bust view, there are still a lot of details in this image. Michael is wearing his dark-blue officer's frock coat, with nine large federal eagle buttons running down the front. With the coat being open, only three of those buttons are visible, along with at least four buttonholes. His shoulder boards have only a gold embroidered border and no interior, besides the dark-blue field. That color also suggests that this image was taken while Michael was the regimental adjutant and thus a staff officer.[329] He has also chosen to add a small personal touch to the image by wearing a non-regulation cravat, while completing his appearance with a new paper color, neatly trimmed mustache and combed hair.

20TH CONNECTICUT INFANTRY

One of eight Connecticut regiments formed following the 1862 call for "300,000 more," the 20th Connecticut Infantry was mustered into Federal service on September 8, 1862. The regiment was made up of seven companies from New Haven County and three from Hartford County. Ordered to Washington on September 11, the regiment received its arms and accoutrements in the national capital. From there, it was sent to Arlington Heights, Virginia, and by the end of the month to Frederick, Maryland. On October 2, the 20th Connecticut was ordered to Harpers Ferry, Virginia, where it was assigned to the XII Corps, Army of the Potomac. From there the 20th Connecticut was sent down the Blue Ridge to guard Keys Gap, where it fought its first skirmish in early November. Not long thereafter, the XII Corps moved to rejoin the Army of the Potomac, taking the 20th Connecticut with it. The XII Corps first moved to Fairfax Station, Virginia, but was ordered into winter quarters at Stafford Court House, Virginia, on January 17, 1863.[330]

On April 27, 1863, the XII Corps crossed the Rappahannock River at Germania Ford, marching for Chancellorsville, Virginia, which was reached three days later. The following day, May 1, the Battle of Chancellorsville began. The 20th Connecticut fought well during its first major engagement and suffered significantly for its stubbornness.[331] Two months later, the XII Corps reached the field of Gettysburg and on July 2 was ordered to take position on the extreme right of the Federal line at Culp's Hill. There the men dug in, developing two distinct lines of defense on lower Culp's Hill that were fought over for much of the rest of the battle.[332] Following the Confederate defeat, the 20th Connecticut was involved in the pursuit of the Army of Northern Virginia back to Virginia. On September 25, the regiment and the XII Corps left Virginia for the Western Theater to join the Army of the Cumberland at Bridgeport, Alabama, on October 3. The 20th Connecticut spent the remainder of 1863 on garrison and fatigue duty.[333]

On April 11, 1864, the 20th Connecticut was transferred to the XX Corps, upon the combining of the old XI and XII Corps. Joining the Military Division of the Mississippi, the XX Corps participated in the advance through northern Georgia that summer and the subsequent Siege of Atlanta. The 20th Connecticut distinguished itself in many engagements that summer and was among the first Federal forces to enter Atlanta, Georgia, following the city's surrender on September 2, 1864. That fall, the 20th Connecticut, as part of the XX Corps, participated in the successful March to the Sea and the Siege of Savannah prior to the Carolinas Campaign over the winter and spring of 1865. The 20th Connecticut continued north and arrived in Washington on May 20, in time to participate in the Grand Review on May 24, 1865. Following the festivities, the regiment encamped near Fort Lincoln and remained there until mustered out of service on June 13, 1865.[334]

Lieutenant Colonel William B. Wooster, who had been captured at Chancellorsville, returned to the 20th Connecticut Infantry in time for Gettysburg and commanded the regiment there.[335] He wrote of the battle:

> *At daybreak on the morning of the 2d instant, we were moved to a position in line of battle on the right, holding the front line, supported by other forces of the brigade.*
>
> *Company B was deployed as skirmishers, and well advanced from the main line. Between 10 and 11 a.m. we were withdrawn, and with the division moved to the Gettysburg road, and thence advanced near to Cemetery Hill, and were placed in position as a support to the Second Division of the Twelfth Army Corps—and we endeavored to return to the position on the right that we had last occupied, but it was found that during our absence the enemy had advance on the right, and gained the breastworks in front and the stone wall, where we had previously been placed as a reserve, and the hills and woods on each side of the wall. At daylight our artillery commenced shelling the woods, breast-works, and locality of the wall formerly held by us, then occupied by the rebels.*
>
> *A little after 5 a.m. my regiment advanced under orders into the edge of the woods. From this position a heavy force of skirmishers proceeded but a few rods to the brow of the hill before they engaged the enemy. From this time for over five hours parts of my regiment were unceasingly engaged with the enemy, the advanced line being frequently relieved from my main line. The enemy were endeavoring to advance through the woods, so as to turn the right flank of the Second Division, and were met and successfully resisted by my regiment. At times it became necessary to advance my left wing to successfully repulse the advancing column of the enemy, and again to retire my whole command to save it from being destroyed by our own artillery. We continued thus advancing and fighting until about 10.30 a.m., when, the rebels having been driven by our fire and shells from the stone wall and breastworks in our front, my regiment steadily advanced in line, and occupied both the wall and breastworks under a continuous fire from sharpshooters in tree-tops, whom we had been unable thus far to silence. Immediately on gaining the breastworks, my regiment was relieved by the One hundred and twenty-third Regt. New York Volunteers.[336]*

Captain William W. Morse

Commanding Company G as it labored on Culp's Hill was Captain William W. Morse. William had previously served as a sergeant in Company G of the 2nd Connecticut Infantry, a three-month regiment that mustered out on August 7, 1861.[337] Reenlisting one year later, William was commissioned as captain of Company G for the 20th Connecticut Infantry on September 8, 1862. Born in New Haven, Connecticut, in 1837 and a bookkeeper before the war, William was still a resident of New Haven at the time of his enlistment. The Company Descriptive Book described him as five feet, nine and a half inches tall, with a light complexion, hazel eyes and brown hair. His service records list him as present until the January/February 1863 report, when he was recorded as absent, having been left sick in Fairfax, Virginia, on January 19, 1863. William returned to duty on March 16, 1863, and remained with his company until February 7, 1864, when he was detached and assigned to the topographical engineers. On May 29, William returned to the regiment and resumed command of Company G. During the summer of 1864, William became sick on July 18 and was sent to a hospital in Marietta, Georgia. On October 10, he was moved to a hospital in Nashville, Tennessee. During his stay, William was remarked upon by another soldier, First Lieutenant George W. Bailey of the 6th Missouri Infantry, in his diary: "Capt. Morse, Twentieth Connecticut Infantry, Twentieth Army Corps.—Not very sick,—not very well; fond of billiards; not fond of hospital or sickness; a free and easy kind of a fellow, bound to take the world easy."[338] At the beginning of November, William was ordered by hospital train to Chattanooga, Tennessee, and to report to the hospital upon arrival. He did so on November 8, 1864, and was admitted with syphilis. William was fortunate to return to duty on November 24, but a mere four days later, he requested a twenty-day leave of absence, which was denied. Still apparently suffering, he applied on December 9, 1864, to move to a hospital in New York. There is no indication in his records whether this was granted. However, his records do show that he was present commanding the company from January 1865 until he mustered out of the service on June 13, 1865, at Fort Lincoln, Washington. He had last been paid on October 31, 1864. William was twice breveted for "Good conduct during the war," first to major, on August 22, 1865, and again to lieutenant colonel on June 22, 1867.[339]

Upon his return to New Haven, William Morse had an extensive career in both politics and entertainment. An expert pool player and an enthusiastic supporter of the game, he opened a billiard hall in New Haven. He also

Left: Captain William Morse, 20th Connecticut Infantry. Back of Morse's image.

sat on the city's board of aldermen and in the late 1870s was New Haven's police commissioner. During this period, William went west for several years and established a billiard hall in Kansas City, Missouri, before returning to New Haven a few years before his passing.[340] In 1898, he was working as an accountant for the New Haven Gas Light Company and on the evening of December 5 was enjoying a game of pool when he was struck with a fainting fit. Taken to his residence, William Wilson Morse passed away at 12:45 a.m. on December 6, 1898.[341] On December 8, William's funeral was attended by his comrades in the Admiral Foote Post of the Grand Army of the Republic, and his casket was escorted to its final resting place at New Haven's Grove Street Cemetery by a platoon of police officers.[342] Although he had never filed for a pension, his widow filed for a survivor's pension on April 11, 1906.[343]

THIS IMAGE WAS TAKEN at the photography studio of Myron A. Filley and C. Gilbert in New Haven, Connecticut. The photographers have used a simple stamp advertisement for their studio, which was just one of several locations on Chapel Street used by Filley and his various partners over the years.[344] The CDV has also been signed on the back, giving William Morse's name, rank regiment and company, suggesting that this was a calling card.

The image itself is rather relaxed, not only in pose but also in dress. William is seated, legs crossed, and has his right arm resting comfortably on a small table that has been provided. His uniform is also that of a soldier who has spent time in the field and has purchased his attire for comfort. William wears the sky-blue trousers that were authorized in General Orders #108; the dark-blue piping running up the seam is clearly visible on his left leg.[345] His coat is an officer's fatigue blouse. Cut long, these had four to five large federal eagle buttons down the front, four being visible here; there would also be smaller eagle buttons on the cuffs. The fatigue blouse was a much looser garment and far less formal than a frock. This design also features an external breast pocket where William appears to have a small handkerchief.[346] His shoulder boards are quite prominent, and the gold embroidered border surrounds a sky-blue field for the infantry with two barely visible captains' bars on each end of the board.

Sitting on the table beside him is his hat. Sometimes referred to as a slouch hat, due to the ability to pin up the sides, this soft felt hat had at least a three-inch brim and six-inch crown, with a half-inch binding around the brim of black ribbed silk. Around the crown is William's black silk and gold hat cord, with acorn finials. His branch of service and regiment are prominently displayed on the front of his hat using a black velvet patch. The border of the patch and the hunter's horn within are gold embroidered, while silver has been used within the loop of the horn for the "20" for the 20th Connecticut Infantry.[347]

William's uniform appears almost pristine in this image, which was most likely taken in the fall of 1862, prior to the 20th Connecticut leaving New Haven for Washington. As a final touch, William Morse has combed back his unruly hair and sports a set of mutton chops with a small goatee. William has already seen limited service by this point and is about to embark on a far more rigorous campaign. As such, he looks directly at the camera with a determined gaze.

123ʳᵈ New York Infantry

In the summer of 1862, Washington County, New York, pledged that it would raise an entire regiment. The men who made up the 123ʳᵈ New York Infantry rendezvoused in Salem, New York, and mustered into United States service on September 4, 1862, for three years. The regiment left the state on September 5, 1862, taking the train to Washington and reached the national capital on September 7. The men filed into camp near Capitol Hill and were eventually sent to Arlington Heights, Virginia. The 123ʳᵈ New York remained in camp drilling and on guard duty until September 29, when the regiment was sent first to Frederick, Maryland, and finally to the Pleasant Valley and Harpers Ferry, Virginia. There the regiment was assigned to the XII Corps and remained as part of the Harpers Ferry garrison until the XII Corps was ordered to rejoin the Army of the Potomac. After a stay in the Loudoun Valley, the regiment eventually went into winter camp at Fairfax Station, Virginia.[348]

In the spring of 1863, the 123ʳᵈ New York fought in the Battle of Chancellorsville. This turned out to be not only the regiment's first but also its bloodiest battle of the war. Later that summer, the 123ʳᵈ New York brought almost five hundred men to Gettysburg but was only limitedly engaged. The New Yorkers joined in the pursuit of Confederate forces back to Virginia and were stationed on the Rappahannock River until September 23, 1863, when the regiment was ordered, with the rest of the XII Corps, to the Western Theater. Upon reaching Tennessee, the XII Corps was transferred to the Army of the Cumberland, and the 123ʳᵈ New York performed guard and picket duty for several months along the Nashville & Chattanooga Railroad. In April 1864, the XI and XII Corps were merged into the XX Corps, joining Major General William T. Sherman's Military Division of the Mississippi on the Atlanta Campaign, the Siege of Atlanta and the March to the Sea. As 1865 dawned, this same command stepped off on the Carolinas Campaign. After the success of that march, Federal forces continued north, arriving in Washington in time to participate in the Grand Review on May 24, 1865. Shortly thereafter, the 123ʳᵈ New York mustered out on June 8, 1865; those members not entitled to be mustered out were transferred to the 145ᵗʰ New York Infantry.[349]

Although the regiment was utilized as a reserve for much of the battle, Lieutenant Colonel James C. Rogers still gave a report of the 123ʳᵈ New York Infantry at Gettysburg:

Next morning we were ordered in position on the hill near Rock Creek. Afterward were moved toward the town, into the woods to the right of Cemetery Hill. Here the regiment, being in the front line of the brigade, built a strong breastwork along its front. About dark it was ordered back to its old ground. On approaching the woods in which the works were located, Company I was sent out as skirmishers, who soon reported the rebels in the works. It lay on its arms until morning, when a battery was planted in its rear to shell the woods in front. One man was killed and 1 wounded by the bursting of the shells of this battery in our ranks. The regiment lay in this position as a reserve until about 2 p.m., when, the enemy having been driven from the breastworks, it moved forward and occupied them.[350]

Second Lieutenant George W. Smith

Helping keep the men of Company B steady during the fighting on Culp's Hill was Second Lieutenant George W. Smith. Born in New York in 1841, George moved to Michigan at a young age and was farming there when the war broke out. Returning to New York, the twenty-year-old enlisted with his uncles and mustered into Company B of the 123rd New York Infantry as a private on August 13, 1862, at Kingsbury, New York. The Company Descriptive Book describes George as five feet, nine inches tall with a dark complexion, blue eyes and dark hair. His service records show him as "present" from September 4, 1862, to April 10, 1863. During this period, George was promoted to first sergeant and received $113 from a Major Paulings, though for what was not specified. The January/February 1863 report shows George as present and entitled to $75 bounty having received $25. On June 10, 1863, at the opening of the Gettysburg Campaign, George was promoted to second lieutenant at Stafford Court House, Virginia. He continued to be present for the rest of his service, except for the March/April 1864 period when his status was not stated. During July/August 1864, George was entitled to an extra $11 per month for commanding Company B starting on August 19, 1864. The next period has the same note that he was due extra pay for commanding the company for September and October. On November 10, 1864, George was detailed as adjutant. On March 27, 1865, he was transferred to Company K and promoted to first lieutenant. George mustered out of the service on June 8, 1865, and was last paid on March 26, 1865.[351]

The history of the 123rd New York mentions that George was twice wounded in the war, once at Gettysburg and again at Dallas, Georgia, in 1864. Referred to as "slight," neither wound was mentioned in his official records. Sadly, this history also notes that George was "murdered in Texas since the war."[352] The details of George's murder relate to the turbulent postwar years in Texas. George had moved to Texas with one of his uncles after the war. There he got involved in Republican politics and was elected to the 1868 Constitutional Convention. That fall, he was in a confrontation with former Confederates where two men were wounded. George turned himself in and was being held in Jefferson, Texas, when, on October 4, 1868, about seventy masked individuals broke into the jail and riddled George and two freedmen who were also present with bullets.[353] Twenty-three men were charged and brought to trial in late May 1869. Three were sentenced to life sentences for murder, with lesser charges for others.[354] It is unknown where George Smith's remains lie today, but there is a cenotaph for him with his parents' headstone at Curtis Cemetery in Bronson, Michigan.[355]

Taken at the Metropolitan Gallery in Washington by John Holyland, this seated image of George Smith was likely taken at the end of his enlistment in the spring of 1865. The stain over the top of the photographer's advertisement on the back is from the original tax stamp adhesive, as the stamp itself was no doubt removed by a collector. The image appears to have been a gift, as it has been signed on both the front and back and, along with identifying the regiment, has been personalized, "Yours Fraternally."

The Metropolitan Gallery provided George with a special chair for this seated image, and the tasseled right arm is specifically designed to help the subject brace. There is a small matching table as well, on which a book, possibly a Bible, was placed. As this was likely one of the last things George did before heading home, he really went all out with his appearance. His uniform, though clean, is also worn, showing the effects of not only time in the field but also George's experience. His trousers are the prewar and early war dark-blue, with the infantry sky-blue piping running up the seam being visible on his left leg. Draped across that same leg is his black leather sword belt, an item that appears to have been repaired. The belt plate is quite prominent and appears to be the standard two-inch-wide rectangular plate with the Arms of the United States on it. The eagle, with its wings spread, can be made out, as can the laurel wreath on either side of the wings.

Left: Lieutenant George Smith, 123rd New York Infantry. *Right*: Back of Smith's image.

Though not visible here, a scroll with the nation's motto, *E Pluribus Unum*, beneath the eagle is also common.[356]

Attached to George's sword belt, and just barely visible, are the inch-wide suspension straps for the sword. The sword is cradled in his left arm and is an excellent example of a Model 1850 field or foot officer's sword. The slightly curved blade, along with the Phrygian helmet pommel, are both indicators, as is the half basket guard, with floral and patriotic designs and the upturned quillon on the counterguard. The grip of the weapon is wood with a fish skin or leather cover wrapped with twisted gilt wire. The blade itself, though not visible, was often etched with patriotic and floral patterns. In this case, most of the scabbard can be seen, with both the brass throat and middle band being visible. The scabbard body is iron and has apparently been allowed to brown, as it does not appear particularly bright in this image.[357]

Beginning at George's waistline is his vest. This dark blue garment has five small federal eagle buttons visible and allowed the coat to be open in public. There is a decorative line running from a buttonhole on the vest back underneath his coat. A twisted cord of some kind, this could be for a watch, as some sort of decorative fob is also hanging off the line. A similar cord can be seen around the crown of George's felt slouch hat. In this case, the cord is black silk with gold and has acorn finials. The half-inch black silk binding around the brim of the hat is also visible, as is the small star on the left side of the crown. This decoration appears dark due to it being a red star for the 1st Division of the XII Corps.[358]

Standing out from the rest of George's uniform is his officer's fatigue blouse or sack coat. As with all officers' uniforms, this was a private purchase, and George has gone for both comfort and style. Not as restrictive as a frock coat, the fatigue blouse was worn in the field. In George's case, his coat is loose, with four large federal eagle buttons running down the front. He opted for a turned-down velvet collar and edged the coat with a black silk binding. For convenience, George has a large pocket on the left side of his coat, which has also been edged and is likely duplicated on his right side.[359] This same black silk has been used for the officer's knot on his sleeve. The braiding on George's left sleeve appears to be those of a captain, two braids with a single knot, as opposed to a single braid and knot of a first lieutenant. His shoulder boards clearly represent the lower rank, as the single gold bar of a first lieutenant can be seen with the sky-blue field on both boards.[360]

As a finishing touch, not only is George wearing a small, non-regulation cravat, but he has also shaved and cut his hair. A final indication as to when this was taken can also be seen on his left sleeve, peeking from behind his sword. George Smith is wearing a mourning ribbon, in all likelihood for the recent assassination of President Abraham Lincoln.

Captain Duncan Robertson

Commanding Company F of the 123rd New York was Captain Duncan Robertson. Duncan had been captain of Company F since he mustered into the service on September 10, 1862, at Salem, New York. Born in 1824 in Argyle, New York, he was thirty-seven years old when he enlisted to serve for three years. Duncan was present for duty starting in September through October 31, 1862. His November/December report, however, showed that his presence was not stated. He was nonetheless listed as present for the entirety of 1863. In January/February 1864, Duncan was detached and sent on recruiting duty in Washington County, New York. He returned to the 123rd New York on May 11, 1864. His May/June report noted that Duncan was due an additional ten dollars per month for commanding Company F during the months of November and December 1863, plus half of January 1864. On April 28, 1865, and again on May 7, 1865, he was appointed "Field officer of the Day" for the brigade. Duncan mustered out on June 8, 1865, in Washington, having last been paid on August 31, 1864.[361]

Duncan returned to Argyle, his lifelong home. Having been a farmer before the war, he continued that vocation. He married Alice Armstrong in the decade before the war, and the couple had two children.[362] Two more children were born after Duncan's return, one surviving childhood.[363] He was also active in the veterans community and was the president of the Washington County Veteran Association, which played a significant role in the annual Sandy Hill, New York reunion that began in 1878.[364] According to his pension card, Duncan filed for a pension on July 20, 1890. Duncan Robertson's date of death was given as August 4, 1899, and he was buried at Greenwich Cemetery, plot G 15, Greenwich, New York.[365] Interestingly, although August 4 is on his headstone, it appears that Duncan died on August 1, 1899, from heart failure.[366] The August 1 date is also used on the New York State Death Index for 1899.[367] After his passing, Alice filed for a survivor's pension on August 28, 1899.[368]

THIS STANDING IMAGE OF Duncan Robertson was taken in Troy, New York, by photographer C.C. Schoonmaker, likely in the late spring of 1864, just before Duncan returned to his regiment after recruiting in New York. The image was apparently used as a calling card by Duncan, as it is signed on the front with his regiment, as well as on the back with his name, rank, regiment and corps. A more recent collector copied that information in pencil near the top of the image. The CDV is very plain, with a blank background and a chair that was provided to brace or rest against. Although the image is cut off, a bit of Duncan's dark-blue trousers are visible. Popular with officers, these early war trousers have the sky-blue piping of the infantry running up the seam.[369] Duncan's large frock coat has skirting that nearly reaches his knees, as well as voluminous sleeves popular with officers throughout the Civil War. It also has a short standing collar, seen in late war frock coats. As he is facing the camera, all nine of the large federal eagle buttons can be seen, as well as three smaller cuff buttons on his left sleeve.[370] Interestingly, this variation on the frock coat has a buttoned loop at Duncan's left hip for his sword belt and was most likely requested when ordered. Just barely visible on his shoulders are his badges of rank, his shoulder boards; the two

Left: Captain Duncan Robertson, 123rd New York Infantry. *Right*: Back of Robertson's image.

gold bars of his captain's rank can barely be made out on the left board. In preparation for this photo, Duncan has tried to control his wavy hair and has conformed to regulation by trimming his beard.[371] He is heading back to the front and looks directly at the camera, resigned to whatever awaits him.

3RD MARYLAND INFANTRY

The organization of the 3rd Maryland Infantry began on June 18, 1861, from two different portions of the state, that of Baltimore and Williamsport, Maryland. The enlistment process proved difficult over the summer of 1861, as secessionist sympathies ran high in eastern Maryland following the Union defeat at First Bull Run. On the other hand, those companies raised in Williamsport included a number of Union men and refugees from Jefferson and Berkeley County, Virginia. The Williamsport companies were designated A, B, C and I, while those from Baltimore were re-designated D,

E, F and G. Companies E, H, I and K were completed using men from the 4th Maryland Infantry and the Baltimore Light Infantry, regiments that had failed to complete their organization. The 3rd Maryland was finally mustered into Federal service on February 17, 1862.[372]

On May 24, 1862, the regiment was ordered to Harpers Ferry and assigned to the II Corps. Shortly thereafter, the II Corps was transferred to Major General John Pope's Army of Virginia, under whom it fought its first battle at Cedar Mountain on August 9, 1862. The 3rd Maryland, along with the rest of the II Corps, was in reserve for the rest of the Northern Virginia Campaign and did not directly participate in Second Bull Run or Chantilly but fell back with the Army of Virginia into the defenses of Washington. Transferred to the Army of the Potomac, the II Corps was re-designated the XII Corps and fought as such through the Maryland Campaign in the fall of 1862. There, the 3rd Maryland, though small in number, distinguishing itself in both the East and West Woods during the Battle of Antietam. The XII Corps retook Harpers Ferry on September 22, 1862, and the 3rd Maryland became part of the garrison. Its men remained at Harpers Ferry until ordered to rejoin the Army of the Potomac near Fredericksburg, Virginia, in early December. Missing the battle, the 3rd Maryland moved with the XII Corps to Fairfax Station, Virginia, where the men began to prepare for winter.[373]

Unfortunately for them, on January 19, 1863, the 3rd Maryland was ordered out of camp and struggled through the infamous "Mud March." After the failure of the march, the men were ordered to Stafford Court House, Virginia, where they went into winter quarters. The following spring, the 3rd Maryland suffered its greatest losses at the Battle of Chancellorsville. It then went on to fight on Culp's Hill at Gettysburg that summer and was involved in the pursuit of Confederate forces back to Virginia. In late September, the XII Corps, the 3rd Maryland included, was transferred to the Western Theater and assigned to the Army of the Cumberland, where the regiment guarded the Nashville & Chattanooga Railroad for the rest of 1863. In February 1864, most of the men of the 3rd Maryland reenlisted and received their thirty-day veterans' furlough home in March. Those who did not reenlist served as supply train and provost guards for the remainder of their service. Those who veteranized returned to service in April 1864 and were assigned to the IX Corps in time to join the Overland Campaign that spring. So, for a brief period in 1864, there were two 3rd Maryland Infantries, one with the Army of the Potomac and one with the Army of the Cumberland. Those with the Army of the Potomac went on to fight through the Overland Campaign, the Siege of Petersburg and the subsequent Appomattox Campaign. Though not present at the surrender of the Army of Northern Virginia, the 3rd Maryland briefly garrisoned Petersburg, as well as guarded the Southside Railroad before returning to Washington to participate in the Grand Review on May 23, 1865. It remained as part of the garrison of the Department of Washington until the end of July and was mustered out at Tennallytown in the District of Columbia on July 31, 1865.[374]

Interestingly, both Colonel Joseph M. Sudsburg and Lieutenant Colonel Gilbert P. Robinson, of the 3rd Maryland Infantry, wrote reports on the regiment's actions after Gettysburg. Robinson's report was filed first, with a subsequent report filed in August by Sudsburg. These documents, however, are ordered with Sudsburg's first in the *Official Records*, no doubt due to his rank.

Following is the report of Colonel Joseph M. Sudsburg, 3rd Maryland Infantry:

> *In compliance with circular of August 12, 1863, I have the honor to report that my regiment was engaged, July 2, at Gettysburg on the extreme right of the line, but in the evening we were ordered to the left, where we remained about one hour, when we returned to occupy our former position, but found the enemy had taken possession.*
>
> *On Friday morning, the 3d, we were held in reserve. At noon we advanced and took our former position. At 2 p.m. we were ordered to the center, where we remained until 4 p.m., when orders were received to move again to the right, when we were drawn up in line of battle behind breastworks, and one company was thrown out as skirmishers.[375]*

Following is the report of Lieutenant Colonel Gilbert P. Robinson, 3rd Maryland Infantry:

> *July 1, marched at 5 a.m. in the direction of Gettysburg, and were detailed as guard to the division ordnance train.*
>
> *On the 2d, were relieved, and joined the brigade. We were in the reserve. The balance of the corps was engaged building breast works.*
>
> *There was heavy fighting all day, extending from right to left.*
>
> *In the evening were ordered to the assistance of the left wing, when the enemy fell back. We were then ordered to return to our former position, but on arriving there found the enemy there, and, after exchanging a few shots, fell back. We were then ordered to lie down for the night.*

July 3, at daylight, our artillery opened fire on our lost breastworks. We were held in reserve, but under fire, all day.

At 3 p.m. we advanced and relieved the Second Division, where we kept up a continual fire with the enemy's sharpshooters.[376]

Lieutenant Colonel Gilbert P. Robinson

Leading half of the 3rd Maryland Infantry into the fight at Culp's Hill was Lieutenant Colonel Gilbert Robinson. Born in Ireland in 1831, Gilbert immigrated to the United States in 1852 and joined the United States Army in 1854. Assigned to Company I, 2nd United States Artillery, he fought in the Third Seminole War in Florida, obtaining the rank of sergeant, and mustered out of the service in 1860.[377] At the outset of the Civil War, he was initially a member of the 1st (West) Virginia Rifles beginning in September 1861. He was present until transferred to the 3rd Maryland on February 16, 1862, as captain of Company C. That June, Gilbert was assigned to court-martial duty at Middletown, Virginia. The next event shown in his service records is that he was "acting Major from Aug. 10, 62." In the September/October 1862 report, it was noted that he was transferred to the field and staff of the 3rd Maryland due to his promotion to major. Gilbert was quickly promoted again on October 27, 1862, to lieutenant colonel. The following year, however, on August 16, 1863, Gilbert was brought up on charges following a heated argument with Assistant Surgeon Edwin Hutchinson. Fortunately, the charges were dropped on August 22.

On February 5, 1864, Gilbert, then commanding the 3rd Maryland, went on his veterans' furlough. The next month, he was reported as commanding Lafayette Barracks in Baltimore, Maryland. Sometime in July/August 1864, he returned to the field and assumed command of the 2nd Brigade, 1st Division, IX Army Corps. He was again on leave in Baltimore from October 15 to November 9, 1864, and returned to command the brigade on December 30, 1864. Gilbert mustered out of the service on July 31, 1865, having last been paid on April 30, 1865. He was breveted colonel as of February 6, 1865, for "Gallant & meritous service during the present campaign before Richmond Va and particularly during the operations on the Weldon Railroad" to date from August 18, 1864.[378]

Gilbert married Margaret Downey in 1858 and had two children prior to the war. By 1880, the couple had six children.[379] To support his growing family, Gilbert went into law enforcement and is listed as a police officer in Hudson City, New Jersey, in the 1870 census. By 1880, Gilbert had been made the clerk of the board of police in Jersey City, a position he held for twenty-five years.[380] Gilbert was also active in multiple veteran and social organizations, including the Zabriski Post of the Grand Army of the Republic, the Military Order of the Loyal Legion and the Free and Accepted Masons Templar Lodge No. 203. On Decoration Day (Memorial Day) 1900, Colonel Robinson was invited to take part in the unveiling of the Maryland Monument at Antietam National Battlefield.[381] Gilbert Robinson retired from the police board on December 30, 1904. Four years later, after a six-month illness, he died on June 23, 1908, and is buried at Arlington Memorial Park in Kearny, New Jersey.[382]

TAKEN BY W.J. MILLER in Baltimore, Maryland, this image was apparently a gift, as Gilbert has inscribed the back, "Fraternally yours" in pencil and signed it in ink. He has also identified his home, Hudson City, New Jersey, while a previous collector has noted his rank, name and regiment. As this

Left: Major Gilbert Robinson, 3rd Maryland Infantry. *Right*: Back of Robinson's image.

image was taken in Baltimore but lacks a tax stamp, it was likely taken in the spring of 1864, when Gilbert was commanding the Lafayette Barracks. If it was taken during his fall leave in Baltimore, it would have had a revenue stamp, as those were used from August 1864 to August 1866.

Gilbert is wearing his dark-blue double-breasted frock coat open with the lapels buttoned back. As he was a part of the regimental command, his frock had two rows of seven large federal eagle buttons running down the front, only one of which is visible in this image. As with all officers' uniforms, this frock coat was privately purchased, and Gilbert has opted for a velvet collar.[383] Additionally, his rank insignia is subdued and lacks the full shoulder board. While this was experimented with as early as 1863 as a way for officers to be less conspicuous in combat, it was not made policy until November 1864.[384]

With his frock coat open, Gilbert's vest is also visible and appears to be either white or buff, two of the colors allowed by regulation. The buttons were supposed to be small federal eagle buttons with the appropriate branch of service, but the number and style of buttons often varied dramatically and the use of civilian vests was not uncommon.[385] As a finishing touch, Gilbert wears a bowtie and a starched or paper collar. His hair has been combed back and oiled, while his magnificent mutton chops and goatee have also been neatly shaped.

WHILE NOT HEAVILY ENGAGED at the fighting for Culp's Hill during the Battle of Gettysburg, Colonel Archibald L. McDougall's brigade did its duty. From building breastworks to racing to other threatened portions of the line and back again, these men were where they were needed throughout July 2 and 3, 1863. Their presence at Culp's Hill on July 3 allowed for the continuous reinforcement of the Federal line and the eventual expulsion of Confederate forces from their toehold on the hill.

The seven men profiled here aided in the effort to regain the Culp's breastworks. They came from five different states to help hold the line at Gettysburg in July 1863. While all of them survived the war, few survived to the twentieth century. Two of these men, Colonel James Selfridge and Second Lieutenant George Smith, died tragically after the war, while Sergeant Michael Donovan lingered for decades and well into the twentieth century in an old soldier's home. The rest went home, raised families and lived their lives, most passing away peacefully near the turn or shortly after the turn of the century. Only one, Private John Alexander, has been lost to history. Fortunately, the efforts of these men and their story at Culp's Hill can never be lost.

Epilogue

The fighting on Culp's Hill on July 2 had been done almost exclusively by Brigadier General George S. Greene's brigade after the majority of the XII Corps was sent south in an attempt to aid the Federal left and center. Difficult terrain, stubborn defenders and stout earthworks saw the repulse of Confederate forces under Major General Edward Johnson that afternoon and evening. Johnson had not been enthusiastic about the assault and described Culp's Hill as "a natural fortification, rendered more formidable by deep entrenchments and thick abatis." Greene's men used these natural and man-made defenses to their utmost; by 10:00 p.m. the assaults were over, with Confederate troops only gaining a slight hold in the Federal works below Greene's position.[386]

All throughout the night, both Union and Confederate reinforcements arrived near Culp's Hill. The Federals intended to advance on July 3, retake their captured works and push any remaining Confederates off the hill. The Confederates were looking to exploit the opening they had made during the previous day's attacks and drive in the Union's right flank as Lieutenant General James Longstreet struck the center of the Federal line. With both sides poised to advance at daybreak, it was Federal forces that struck first. Making good on Brigadier General Alpheus Williams's intention to "shell the hell out of them," the Union guns opened around 4:30 a.m. on July 3, 1863.[387]

This bombardment began a nearly seven-hour struggle for Culp's Hill and the Federal right flank. With the return of the rest of the XII Corps, those positions that had held on July 2 were reinforced, while others moved against the Confederates who had gained a portion of the breastworks. The Federal line was also extended south, down the Baltimore Pike to the area of Spangler's Spring, further discouraging Confederate efforts to wrap around the Union right. By 10:30 a.m., the furious contest had ended with the repulse of Confederate forces along the XII Corps' entire front. Culp's Hill, and the Union flank, was secure.

The relative quiet that descended after the Confederate withdrawal was shattered around 1:00 p.m. with the bombardment of the Federal center by approximately 150 Confederate cannons, heralding the beginning of what became the Civil War's most famous charge. All the men on Culp's Hill could do was listen to the roar of the guns and the subsequent crash of musketry in the distance. They also had to take cover from the overshot that was falling into their lines. The thunder of guns both large and small was soon replaced by cheering, the Yankee huzzah, being carried from one regiment to the next, up and down the Federal line. The attack had been broken and the Confederate army repulsed on all fronts.[388]

The fighting at Culp's Hill, while not as well remembered as other parts of the Gettysburg battlefield, saw its own share of bloodshed. The XII Corps sustained 1,082 casualties defending the hill and its immediate area, 204 of those men being killed in action. The Confederate attackers suffered far worse, and their stated 1,823 casualties is thought to be significantly lower than their actual losses.[389] Beyond the human cost, the effect of the intense musketry and artillery fire in such a limited area continued to be visible for years in the dead and dying trees on Culp's Hill.[390]

Today, this unique battlefield landscape is maintained by the National Park Service at Gettysburg National Military Park. Culp's Hill can be accessed by either the driving tour or trails and is dotted with the monuments of the Union regiments that held it. Remnants of the breastworks, as well as the remains of the post-battle mass graves, can still be seen on the hillside. The National Park Service has recently made efforts to return the landscape on and around Culp's Hill to its 1863 appearance by clearing much of the underbrush from the wooded hillside. It is hoped that with these improvements to the view shed, the public will take advantage of this and walk in the footsteps of those who struggled here 160 years ago.

Regiments Engaged at Culp's Hill

The 78th New York reported on June 30, 1863, 8 officers and 194 enlisted men present, total 202. The number reported engaged was 198.[391] Regimental losses were 6 killed, 21 wounded and 3 missing totaling 30 casualties.[392] The regiment was mainly equipped with Enfield .577 rifles.[393]

The 60th New York reported on June 30, 1863, 14 officers and 299 enlisted men present. The number reported engaged was 273.[394] Regimental losses were 11 killed, 41 wounded, 0 missing totaling 52 casualties.[395] The regiment reported they were equipped with Enfield .577 rifle muskets.[396]

The 102nd New York reported on June 30, 1863, 16 officers and 232 enlisted men present, total 248. The number reported engaged was 230.[397] Regimental losses were 4 killed, 17 wounded, 8 missing totaling 29 casualties.[398] By June 30, the regiment was equipped with .58 rifle muskets.[399]

The 137th New York reported on June 30, 1863, 24 officers and 432 enlisted men present, total 456. The number reported engaged 423.[400] Regimental losses were 40 killed, 87 wounded, 10 missing totaling 137 casualties.[401] The regiment was equipped with Enfield .577 rifle muskets.[402]

The 7th Ohio reported on June 30, 1863, 17 officers and 276 enlisted men present, total 293. The number reported engaged was 282.[403] Regimental losses were 1 killed, 17 wounded, 0 missing totaling 18 casualties.[404] The regiment was equipped with .58 rifle muskets of several makers.[405]

The 28th Pennsylvania reported on June 30, 1863, 17 officers and 312 enlisted men present, total 329. The number reported engaged was 303.[406] Regimental losses, 3 killed, 23 wounded 2 missing totaling 28 casualties.[407] Some companies were equipped with .58 rifle muskets, while others had Enfield .577 rifles.[408]

The 5th Ohio reported on June 30, 1863, 18 officers and 297 enlisted men present, total 315. The number reported engaged was 299.[409] Regimental losses, 2 killed, 16 wounded, 0 missing totaling 18 casualties.[410] The regiment was equipped with .58 rifle muskets from various makers.[411]

The 66th Ohio reported on June 30, 1863, 26 officers and 290 enlisted men present, total 316. The number engaged was 299.[412] Regimental losses, 0 killed, 17 wounded, 0 missing totaling 17 casualties.[413] The regiment was equipped with .58 rifle muskets from various makers.[414]

The 2nd Massachusetts reported on June 30, 1863, 27 officers and 370 enlisted men present, total 397. The number engaged was 316.[415] Regimental losses, 23 killed, 109 wounded, 4 missing totaling 136 casualties.[416] The regiment was equipped with the Enfield .577 rifle musket.[417]

The 27th Indiana reported on June 30, 1863, 24 officers and 363 enlisted men present, total 387. The number engaged was 339.[418] Regimental losses, 23 killed, 86 wounded, 1 missing totaling 110 casualties.[419] Several companies were equipped with the .58 rifle musket, while others had the Austrian .58 rifles.[420]

The 107th New York reported on June 30, 1863, 26 officers and 320 enlisted men present, total 346. The number engaged was 319.[421] Regimental losses, 0 killed, 2 wounded, 0 missing totaling 2 casualties.[422] The regiment was equipped with .58 rifle muskets from various makers.[423]

Battery M, 1st New York Light Artillery, reported on June 30, 1863, 4 officers and 93 enlisted men present, total 97. The number engaged was 90.[424] Regimental losses, 0 killed 0 wounded 0 missing totaling 0 casualties.[425] The battery's cannons were four ten-pounder Parrott rifles.[426]

The 46th Pennsylvania reported on June 30, 1863, 24 officers and 272 enlisted men present, total 296. The number engaged was 262.[427] Regimental losses,

2 killed, 10 wounded, 1 missing totaling 13 casualties.[428] The regiment was equipped with .58 rifle muskets from various makers.[429]

The 5th Connecticut reported on June 30, 1863, 16 officers and 302 enlisted men present, total 318. The number engaged was 221.[430] Regimental losses, 0 killed, 2 wounded, 5 missing totaling 7 casualties.[431] The regiment was equipped with .58 rifle muskets from various makers.[432]

The 20th Connecticut reported on June 30, 1863, 20 officers and 360 enlisted men present, total 380. The number engaged was 321.[433] Regimental losses, 5 killed, 22 wounded, 1 missing totaling 28 casualties.[434] The regiment was equipped with .58 rifle muskets.[435]

The 123rd New York reported on June 30, 1863, 26 officers and 446 enlisted men present, total 472. The number engaged was 495.[436] Regimental losses, 3 killed, 10 wounded, 1 missing totaling 14 casualties.[437] The regiment was equipped with both the .58 rifle musket and the Enfield .577 rifle musket.[438]

The 3rd Maryland Infantry reported on June 30, 1863, 12 officers and 230 enlisted men present, total 242. A significant number of troops must have rejoined the ranks, as the number engaged was 290.[439] Regimental losses, 1 killed, 7 wounded, 0 missing totaling 8 casualties.[440] The regiment was equipped with both the standard .58 rifle musket and the Enfield .577 rifle musket.[441]

NOTES

Introduction

1. Darrah, *Cartes de Visite*, 87.

Chapter 1

2. Gottfried, *Brigades of Gettysburg*, 387–88.
3. Stewart, Holloway, Grierson and Pierce, *Union Army*, 2:108.
4. Phisterer, *New York in the War of the Rebellion*, 436.
5. Dyer, *Compendium of the War of the Rebellion*, 3:1,435.
6. Stewart, Holloway, Grierson and Pierce, *Union Army*, 2:108.
7. Dyer, *Compendium of the War of the Rebellion*, 3:1,435 and 1,445.
8. *War of the Rebellion: A Compilation of the Official Records of the Union and Confederate Armies*, series I, vol. 27, part 1, 863–64 (hereafter *OR*).
9. *Democrat & Chronicle*, "Dr. Skinner, 83, Noted Le Roy Surgeon, Dies," 3.
10. National Archives, Military Service Records, Scott Skinner.
11. Fold 3, New York Civil War Muster Roll Abstracts.
12. *Democrat & Chronicle*, "Dr. Skinner, 83, Noted Le Roy Surgeon, Dies," 3.
13. *Buffalo Evening News*, "Dr. Scott W. Skinner Dies at Le Roy," 3; *Democrat & Chronicle*, "Dr. Skinner, 83, Noted Le Roy Surgeon, Dies," 3.
14. Darrah, *Cartes de Visite*, 30.
15. Todd, *American Military Equipage*, 1:70–71.
16. O'Brien and Diefendorf, *General Orders of the War Department*, 1:217.
17. U.S. War Department, *Revised United States Army Regulations of 1861*, 465.
18. Todd, *American Military Equipage*, 1:56.
19. U.S. War Department, *Revised United States Army Regulations of 1861*, 463.
20. Tice, *Uniform Buttons of the United States*, 382–86.
21. U.S. War Department, *Revised United States Army Regulations of 1861*, 468–69.
22. Todd, *American Military Equipage*, 1:177–78, 1:228–29.
23. Woodhead, *Echoes of Glory*, 76–77; Todd, *American Military Equipage*, 1:177–78.

24. U.S. War Department, *Revised United States Army Regulations of 1861*, 481.
25. Eddy, *History of the Sixtieth Regiment*, 12.
26. Phisterer, *New York in the War of the Rebellion*, 420.
27. Stewart, Holloway, Grierson and Pierce, *Union Army*, 2:94.
28. Phisterer, *New York in the War of the Rebellion*, 420.
29. Eddy, *History of the Sixtieth Regiment*, 285–87, 290.
30. Stewart, Holloway, Grierson and Pierce, *Union Army*, 2:94.
31. *OR*, series I, vol. 27, part 1, 860–61.
32. Fold 3, New York Civil War Muster Roll Abstracts; American Civil War Research Database, "Frederick Winslow," Civil War Database.
33. National Archives, Military Service Records, Frederick Winslow.
34. Eddy, *History of the Sixtieth Regiment*, 342; *La Crosse Tribune*, "Retired Merchant, 89, Is Dead at Janesville," 14.
35. National Archives, Military Service Records, Frederick Winslow.
36. *La Crosse Tribune*, "Retired Merchant, 89, Is Dead at Janesville," 14, Find A Grave, Frederick S. Winslow (1840–1930).
37. National Archives and Records Administration, Pension Card Index, Winslow, Frederick S.
38. Find A Grave, Frederick S. Winslow (1840–1930).
39. Eddy, *History of the Sixtieth Regiment*, 5.
40. Darrah, *Cartes de Visite*, 31.
41. O'Brien and Diefendorf, *General Orders of the War Department*, 1:217.
42. Woodhead, *Echoes of Glory*, 127.
43. Todd, *American Military Equipage*, 1:56.
44. *OR*, series I, vol. 25, part 2, 152.
45. U.S. War Department, *Revised United States Army Regulations of 1861*, 481.
46. American Civil War Research Database, "Eugene Diven," Civil War Database; Find A Grave, Eugene Diven (1843–1888).
47. National Archives, Military Service Records, Eugene Diven.
48. Find A Grave, Eugene Diven (1843–1888).
49. National Archives and Records Administration, Pension Card Index, Diven, Eugene; *Mansfield Advisor*, "Chemung County," 2.
50. Todd, *American Military Equipage*, 1:52–54.
51. U.S. War Department, *Revised United States Army Regulations of 1861*, 473–74.
52. Todd, *American Military Equipage*, 1:98.
53. U.S. War Department, *Revised United States Army Regulations of 1861*, 465–66.
54. Debevoise, *Gilbert Molleson Elliott*, 38–39.
55. Stewart, Holloway, Grierson and Pierce, *Union Army*, 2:123.
56. Phisterer, *New York in the War of the Rebellion*, 456.
57. Stewart, Holloway, Grierson and Pierce, *Union Army*, 2:123.
58. *OR*, series I, vol. 27, part 1, 864–66.
59. Debevoise, *Gilbert Molleson Elliott*, 14–16, 37–38.
60. National Archives, Military Service Records, Gilbert Molleson Elliot.
61. Debevoise, *Gilbert Molleson Elliott*, 137–38.
62. *OR*, series I, vol. 27, part 3, 804.

63. Debevoise, *Gilbert Molleson Elliott*, 176, 183–84.

64. National Archives, Military Service Records, Gilbert Molleson Elliot.

65. *New York Daily Herald*, "Late Major Gilbert M. Elliott," 5.

66. Debevoise, *Gilbert Molleson Elliott*, 184.

67. National Archives and Records Administration, Pension Card Index.

68. Todd, *American Military Equipage*, 1:70.

69. U.S. War Department, *Revised United States Army Regulations of 1861*, 468.

70. Todd, *American Military Equipage*, 1:179.

71. U.S. War Department, *Revised United States Army Regulations of 1861*, 467.

72. Peckham, *History of Cornelis Maessen Van Buren*, 183.

73. National Archives, Military Service Records, Barent Van Buren.

74. American Civil War Research Database, "Barent Van Buren," Civil War Database.

75. Peckham, *History of Cornelis Maessen Van Buren*, 184; Find A Grave, Colonel Barent Van Buren (1840–1921).

76. National Archives and Records Administration, Pension Card Index, Van Buren, Barent.

77. *Chicago Daily Tribune*, "Van Buren," 19; Peckham, *History of Cornelis Maessen Van Buren*, 184.

78. Darrah, *Cartes de Visite*, 19.

79. Todd, *American Military Equipage*, 1:72–74.

80. O'Brien and Diefendorf, *General Orders of the War Department*, 1:177.

81. U.S. War Department, *Revised United States Army Regulations of 1861*, 467.

82. Cleutz, *Fields of Fame & Glory*, 31 and 33.

83. Stewart, Holloway, Grierson and Pierce, *Union Army*, 2:148.

84. Fox, *New York at Gettysburg*, 3:938–41.

85. Stewart, Holloway, Grierson and Pierce, *Union Army*, 2:148.

86. *OR*, series I, vol. 27, part 1, 866–67.

87. National Archives, Military Service Records, William A. Scofield.

88. Ibid.

89. Phisterer, *New York in the War of the Rebellion*, 355.

90. Ancestry, *1870 United States Federal Census*.

91. Ancestry, *New York, U.S., State Census, 1875*.

92. National Archives and Records Administration, Pension Card Index, Scofield, William A.

93. Darrah, *Cartes de Visite*, 87.

94. Tice, *Uniform Buttons of the United States*, 382–86; Woodhead, *Echoes of Glory*, 101.

95. U.S. War Department, *Revised United States Army Regulations of 1861*, 467.

96. Fold 3, New York Civil War Muster Roll, 1861–1900, 867 and 869.

97. *Independent-Record*, "George W.P. Pew Dead," 5.

98. National Archives, Military Service Records, George W. Pew.

99. *Butte Inter Mountain*, "Sale of Purebred Stock in Helena on May 6," 3.

100. National Archives and Records Administration, Pension Card Index, Pew, George W.P.; *Great Falls Tribune*, "Pensions for Montanans," 5.

101. Find A Grave, Lieutenant George W.P. Pew (1831–1904); *Independent-Record*, "George W.P. Pew Dead," 5.

102. Todd, *American Military Equipage*, 1:56.
103. U.S. War Department, *Revised United States Army Regulations of 1861*, 464.
104. *OR*, series I, vol. 25, part 2, 152.

Chapter 2

105. Gottfried, *Brigades of Gettysburg*, 378.
106. Ibid., 379.
107. Wilson, *Itinerary of the Seventh Ohio Volunteer Infantry*, 36 and 38.
108. Stewart, Holloway, Grierson and Pierce, *Union Army*, 2:359–60.
109. Wilson, *Itinerary of the Seventh Ohio Volunteer Infantry*, 239.
110. Gottfried, *Brigades of Gettysburg*, 379–80.
111. Stewart, Holloway, Grierson and Pierce, *Union Army*, 2:359–60.
112. Wilson, *Itinerary of the Seventh Ohio Volunteer Infantry*, 366.
113. Ibid., 35–36.
114. National Archives, Military Service Records, William R. Creighton.
115. Wilson, *Itinerary of the Seventh Ohio Volunteer Infantry*, 285–86, 367.
116. *Cleveland Daily Leader*, "The Funeral," 3.
117. Find A Grave, William R. Creighton (1837–1863).
118. Todd, *American Military Equipage*, 1:98, 103.
119. U.S. War Department, *Revised United States Army Regulations of 1861*, 462–63.
120. Todd, *American Military Equipage*, 1:66, 106.
121. Wilson, *Itinerary of the Seventh Ohio Volunteer Infantry*, 370.
122. National Archives, Military Service Records, Orrin J. Crane.
123. National Archives and Records Administration, Pension Card Index, Crane, Orrin J.; *Cleveland Daily Leader*, "Public Proceedings," 3.
124. Wilson, *Itinerary of the Seventh Ohio Volunteer Infantry*, 285–86.
125. Hunt, *Colonels in Blue*, 43.
126. Find A Grave, William R. Creighton (1837–1863).
127. Find A Grave, Orrin J. Crane (1828–1863).
128. U.S. War Department, *Revised United States Army Regulations of 1861*, 471–72.
129. Nicholson, *Re-Union of the 28ᵗʰ & 147ᵗʰ Regiments*, 3–4.
130. Orr, *Last to Leave the Field*, 26 and 52.
131. Stewart, Holloway, Grierson and Pierce, *Union Army*, 1:367–68.
132. Bates, *History of Pennsylvania Volunteers*, 1:426.
133. *OR*, series I, vol. 27, part 1, 184.
134. Stewart, Holloway, Grierson and Pierce, *Union Army*, 1:367–68.
135. *OR*, series I, vol. 27, part 1, 845.
136. Find A Grave, Dr. Henry Earnest Goodman (1836–1896).
137. *Philadelphia Enquirer*, "Earnest Goodman Suddenly Expires," 7.
138. National Archives, Military Service Records, Henry E. Goodman.
139. Historic Marker Database, "Field Hospitals—Twelfth Corps Medical Department."
140. Adjutant General's Office, *Official Army Register for 1865*, 73.
141. National Archives, Military Service Records, Henry E. Goodman; *Philadelphia Enquirer*, "Earnest Goodman Suddenly Expires," 7.

142. Find A Grave, Dr. Henry Earnest Goodman (1836–1896); *Philadelphia Enquirer*, "Earnest Goodman Suddenly Expires," 7; *Philadelphia Times*, "Dr. Goodman's Fatal Run," 2.

143. U.S. War Department, *Revised United States Army Regulations of 1861*, 462–63.

144. O'Brien and Diefendorf, *General Orders of the War Department*, 1:14.

145. U.S. War Department, *Revised United States Army Regulations of 1861*, 481.

146. *York Dispatch*, "Captain Spink," 8.

147. FamilySearch, United States Census, 1860, A. Spinck.

148. American Civil War Research Database, "Arnold B. Spink," Civil War Database.

149. National Archives, Military Service Records, Arnold B. Spink.

150. *Harrisburg Daily Independent*, "Captain Spink Dead," 7.

151. Find A Grave, Arnold Bowen Spink (1842–1912).

152. *Harrisburg Telegraph*, "Full Military Honors for Late Capt. Spink," 9.

153. Find A Grave, Arnold Bowen Spink (1842–1912); *Harrisburg Daily Independent*, "Captain Spink Dead," 7; *Harrisburg Telegraph*, "Full Military Honors for Late Capt. Spink," 9; *Harrisburg Telegraph*, "Captain Spink Victim of Cancer," 3; *York Dispatch*, "Captain Spink," 8.

154. Clark, *19th Century Card Photos Kwik Guide*, 18, 21.

155. Woodhead, *Echoes of Glory*, 190–91.

156. O'Brien and Diefendorf, *General Orders of the War Department*, 1:217; U.S. War Department, *Revised United States Army Regulations of 1861*, 465.

157. U.S. War Department, *Revised United States Army Regulations of 1861*, 465.

158. Todd, *American Military Equipage*, 1:51, 106–7.

159. U.S. War Department, *Revised United States Army Regulations of 1861*, 462.

160. *OR*, series I, vol. 25, part 2, 152.

161. Todd, *American Military Equipage*, 1:66.

162. Reid, *Ohio in the War*, 2:42.

163. Stewart, Holloway, Grierson and Pierce, *Union Army*, 2:356–57.

164. Reid, *Ohio in the War*, 2:44.

165. Paver, *What I Saw from 1861 to 1864*, 31–32.

166. Reid, *Ohio in the War*, 2:44.

167. Paver, *What I Saw from 1861 to 1864*, 33–36.

168. Stewart, Holloway, Grierson and Pierce, *Union Army*, 2:356–57.

169. *OR*, series I, vol. 27, part 1, 839–40.

170. National Archives, Military Service Records, Wilson B. Gaither.

171. Ancestry, *Ohio, U.S., County Marriage Records, 1774–1993*.

172. Ancestry, *U.S., City Directories, 1822–1995*; Find A Grave, Captain Wilson B. Gaither (1839–1872).

173. National Archives and Records Administration, Pension Card Index, Gaither, Wilson B.

174. Find A Grave, Captain Wilson B. Gaither (1839–1872); Find A Grave, 5th Ohio Volunteer Infantry Memorial.

175. Clark, *19th Century Card Photos Kwik Guide*, 23.

176. Woodhead, *Echoes of Glory*, 116–17.

177. National Archives, Military Service Records, Mathias Schwab.

178. Cincinnati Fire Department History, "Captain Mathias Schwab."
179. Find A Grave, Captain Mathias Schwab (1840–1869).
180. Reid, *Ohio in the War*, 2:46.
181. Clark, *19th Century Card Photos Kwik Guide*, 21 and 23.
182. Woodhead, *Echoes of Glory*, 175.
183. U.S. War Department, *Revised United States Army Regulations of 1861*, 467.
184. Reid, *Ohio in the War*, 2:387–88.
185. Stewart, Holloway, Grierson and Pierce, *Union Army*, 2:400.
186. *OR*, series I, vol. 27, part 1, 844–45.
187. Find A Grave, John William Watkins (1838–1899).
188. National Archives, Military Service Records, John W. Watkins.
189. General Information about the Ohio Girls Industrial School; Find A Grave, John William Watkins (1838–1899); *Marion (OH) Star*, "Captain Watkins," 4.
190. National Archives and Records Administration, Pension Card Index, Watkins, John W.; *Marion (OH) Star*, "Captain Watkins," 4; *Marion (OH) Star*, "Burials," 8.
191. U.S. War Department, *Revised United States Army Regulations of 1861*, 465.
192. Todd, *American Military Equipage*, 1:66.
193. *OR*, series I, vol. 25, part 2, 152.
194. Pfanz, *Gettysburg*, 351–52.

Chapter 3

195. Gottfried, *Brigades of Gettysburg*, 365.
196. Pfanz, *Gettysburg*, 341; Quint, *Record of the Second Massachusetts Infantry*, 194 and 204.
197. Quint, *Record of the Second Massachusetts Infantry*, 10, 14, 21, 32.
198. Stewart, Holloway, Grierson and Pierce, *Union Army*, 1:168–69.
199. *OR*, series I, vol. 27, part 1, 816–17.
200. Quint, *Record of the Second Massachusetts Infantry*, 479; Find A Grave, Dr. William H. Heath (1828–1864).
201. National Archives and Records Administration, Compiled Service Records, 17; Quint, *Record of the Second Massachusetts Infantry*, 479.
202. National Archives and Records Administration, Compiled Service Records, 17.
203. Find A Grave, Dr. William H. Heath (1828–1864).
204. National Archives and Records Administration, Pension Card Index, Heath, William H.
205. Darrah, *Cartes de Visite*, 19.
206. U.S. War Department, *Revised United States Army Regulations of 1861*, 462–63.
207. Quint, *Record of the Second Massachusetts Infantry*, 505.
208. National Archives and Records Administration, Compiled Service Records, 3.
209. *Boston Globe*, "A Striking Story," 8; *Boston Post*, "At the Point of Pines," 1.
210. Find A Grave, Lieutenant Albert W Mann (1836–1881).
211. National Archives and Records Administration, Pension Card Index, Mann, Albert W.
212. U.S. War Department, *Revised United States Army Regulations of 1861*, 464.

213. Todd, *American Military Equipage*, 1:104.

214. Collection of Matthew Borders; Todd, *American Military Equipage*, 1:222.

215. U.S. War Department, *Revised United States Army Regulations of 1861*, 481.

216. *Boston Globe*, "Funeral of Maj John A. Fox Tomorrow Afternoon," 16.

217. Quint, *Record of the Second Massachusetts Infantry*, 498.

218. Pfanz, *Gettysburg*, 180.

219. National Archives, Military Service Records, John A. Fox.

220. Massachusetts Historical Society, "Fox Family Papers"; *Boston Globe*, "Funeral of Maj John A. Fox Tomorrow Afternoon," 16.

221. Find A Grave, John Andrews Fox (1835–1920); *Boston Globe*, "Dorchester District," 11.

222. National Archives and Records Administration, Pension Card Index, Fox, John A.

223. O'Brien and Diefendorf, *General Orders of the War Department*, 1:217.

224. Todd, *American Military Equipage*, 1:57–58.

225. U.S. War Department, *Revised United States Army Regulations of 1861*, 471–72.

226. Woodhead, *Echoes of Glory*, 180.

227. Brown, *Twenty-Seventh Indiana Volunteer Infantry*, 13, 26, 42–43.

228. Stewart, Holloway, Grierson and Pierce, *Union Army*, 3:127.

229. Brown, *Twenty-Seventh Indiana Volunteer Infantry*, 184, 194, 225.

230. Carman, *Maryland Campaign of September 1862*, 1:279–81.

231. Brown, *Twenty-Seventh Indiana Volunteer Infantry*, 416.

232. Stewart, Holloway, Grierson and Pierce, *Union Army*, 3:127–28.

233. *OR*, series I, vol. 27, part 1, 815–16.

234. Find A Grave, Peter Ragle Jr. (1842–1918).

235. National Archives, Military Service Records, Peter Ragle Jr.

236. Civil War Veterans, "Ragle, Peter"; Brown, *Twenty-Seventh Indiana Volunteer Infantry*, 384.

237. Brown, *Twenty-Seventh Indiana Volunteer Infantry*, 454.

238. National Archives, Military Service Records, Peter Ragle Jr.

239. Ibid.

240. Brown, *Twenty-Seventh Indiana Volunteer Infantry*, 479.

241. National Archives, Military Service Records, Peter Ragle Jr.

242. National Archives and Records Administration, Pension Card Index, Ragle, Peter.

243. Find A Grave, Peter Ragle Jr. (1842–1918); Rootsweb, "Trueblood Family in America."

244. *Boonville Enquirer*, "Short Treasurers," 2; *Indianapolis Journal*, "Martin County Auditorship," 2; *Martin County Democrat*, "Recount Concluded," 1; *Indianapolis Journal*, "Indiana Notes," 5.

245. 1910 Census, Place: Elmore Daviess, Indiana; Roll: T624_344; Page: 4A; Find A Grave, "Peter Ragle Jr."

246. U.S. War Department, *Revised United States Army Regulations of 1861*, 467.

247. *Hartford Courant*, "107th New York Regiment," 2.

248. Stewart, Holloway, Grierson and Pierce, *Union Army*, 2:127.

249. Tuttle, *Civil War Journal of Lt. Russell M. Tuttle*, 18–20.

250. Stewart, Holloway, Grierson and Pierce, *Union Army*, 2:128.

251. Weller, *Civil War Courtship*, 50–51 and 54.

252. Stewart, Holloway, Grierson and Pierce, *Union Army*, 2:128.

253. *OR*, series I, vol. 27, part 1, 819–21.

254. National Archives, Military Service Records, Edwin G. Fay.

255. *Star-Gazette*, "Edwin G. Fay," June 14, 1902, 5.

256. National Archives, Military Service Records, Edwin G. Fay.

257. FamilySearch, United States Census, 1900.

258. *Philadelphia Enquirer*, "Quarrel Between Partners," 2.

259. *Philadelphia Enquirer*, "Loyal Legion," 3; *Star-Gazette*, "Personal," 7; *Star-Gazette*, "107th N.Y. VOLS," 5, 7.

260. National Archives and Records Administration, Pension Card Index, Fay, Edwin G.

261. *Star-Gazette*, "Edwin G. Fry," June 16, 1902, 7; Find A Grave, Edwin Gould Fay (1841–1902).

262. Tice, *Uniform Buttons of the United States*, 385–86.

263. *Star-Gazette*, "Taps Sound for Captain Frank P. Frost," 5.

264. National Archives, Military Service Records, Frank Frost.

265. *Star-Gazette*, "Taps Sound for Captain Frank P. Frost," 5.

266. National Archives, Military Service Records, Frank Frost.

267. Find A Grave, CPT Frank Pomeroy Frost (1841–1934); *Star-Gazette*, "Taps Sound for Captain Frank P. Frost," 5.

268. *Star-Gazette*, "Capt. Frank P. Frost," November 5, 1934, 17.

269. *Star-Gazette*, "Just Chat," 3.

270. National Archives and Records Administration, Pension Card Index, Frost, Frank P.

271. Find A Grave, CPT Frank Pomeroy Frost (1841–1934); *Star-Gazette*, "Capt. Frank P. Frost," November 5, 1934, 17; *Star-Gazette*, "Capt. Frank P. Frost," November 6, 1934, 6.

272. *Star-Gazette*, "Taps Sound for Captain Frank P. Frost," 5.

273. Clark, *19th Century Card Photos Kwik Guide*, 23–24.

274. Fox, *New York at Gettysburg*, 3:1,263.

275. Stewart, Holloway, Grierson and Pierce, *Union Army*, 2:208.

276. Fox, *New York at Gettysburg*, 3:1,265.

277. Ibid., 1,266.

278. Stewart, Holloway, Grierson and Pierce, *Union Army*, 2:208.

279. Pfanz, *Gettysburg*, 331, 334.

280. Find A Grave, Private Martin H. Schuck (1838–1915).

281. National Archives, Military Service Records, Martin H. Schuck.

282. FamilySearch, United States Census, 1880, image 30 of 35.

283. National Archives and Records Administration, Pension Card Index, Schuck, Martin H.

284. FamilySearch, New York, State Death Index, 1880–1956.

285. Find A Grave, Private Martin H. Schuck (1838–1915).

286. U.S. War Department, *Revised United States Army Regulations of 1861*, 463–64.

287. Todd, *American Military Equipage*, 1:52–53.
288. *OR*, series I, vol. 25, part 2, 152.

Chapter 4

289. Gottfried, *Brigades of Gettysburg*, 354–55.
290. Pfanz, *Gettysburg*, 198, 230–34; Gottfried, *Brigades of Gettysburg*, 355.
291. Gottfried, *Maps of Gettysburg*, 248–49.
292. Stewart, Holloway, Grierson and Pierce, *Union Army*, 1:379.
293. Bates, *History of Pennsylvania Volunteers*, 1:1,112–14.
294. Stewart, Holloway, Grierson and Pierce, *Union Army*, 1:379.
295. *OR*, series I, vol. 27, part 1, 802–3.
296. Coffin, *Record of the Men of Lafayette*, 178.
297. National Archives, Military Service Records, James L. Selfridge.
298. *Philadelphia Times*, "Old Soldier's Suicide," 1.
299. *Lancaster Examiner*, "Soldier's Suicide," 3.
300. *Philadelphia Times*, "Old Soldier's Suicide," 1.
301. National Archives and Records Administration, Pension Card Index, Selfridge, James L.
302. Find A Grave, General James Lercon Selfridge (1824–1887).
303. U.S. War Department, *Revised United States Army Regulations of 1861*, 462–63; Todd, *American Military Equipage*, 1:107–8.
304. U.S. War Department, *Revised United States Army Regulations of 1861*, 471–72; Todd, *American Military Equipage*, 1:98.
305. U.S. War Department, *Revised United States Army Regulations of 1861*, 467 and 481.
306. Marvin, *Fifth Regiment Connecticut Volunteers*, 19–23 and 25.
307. Smith, Camp and Barbour, *Record of Service of Connecticut Men*, 220–21.
308. Marvin, *Fifth Regiment Connecticut Volunteers*, 79, 91–93.
309. Smith, Camp and Barbour, *Record of Service of Connecticut Men*, 221–22.
310. Ibid., 222.
311. Stewart, Holloway, Grierson and Pierce, *Union Army*, 1:277.
312. Smith, Camp and Barbour, *Record of Service of Connecticut Men*, 222–23.
313. *OR*, series I, vol. 27, part 1, 788–89.
314. National Archives, Military Service Records, John Alexander.
315. National Archives, Special Schedules of the Eleventh Census.
316. Monument Committee, *Fifth Connecticut Volunteers*, 25.
317. National Archives and Records Administration, Pension Card Index, Alexander, John; FamilySearch, United States Census of Union Veterans and Widows of the Civil War, 1890.
318. Clark, *19th Century Card Photos Kwik Guide*, 18 and 21.
319. O'Brien and Diefendorf, *General Orders of the War Department*, 1:217.
320. U.S. War Department, *Revised United States Army Regulations of 1861*, 463.
321. Lord, *Civil War Collector's Encyclopedia*, 296.
322. Todd, *American Military Equipage*, 1:62–64.
323. National Archives, Military Service Records, Michael Donovan.

324. FamilySearch, California, County Birth and Death Records, 1800–1994.
325. National Archives and Records Administration, Pension Card Index, Donovan, Michael.
326. FamilySearch, California, County Birth and Death Records, 1800–1994.
327. Find A Grave, Michael Donovan (unknown–1929).
328. Darrah, *Cartes de Visite*, 19.
329. U.S. War Department, *Revised United States Army Regulations of 1861*, 471.
330. Smith, Camp and Barbour, *Record of Service of Connecticut Men*, 690.
331. Storrs, *"Twentieth Connecticut,"* 44–46, 50–52.
332. Gottfried, *Brigades of Gettysburg*, 354–55.
333. Stewart, Holloway, Grierson and Pierce, *Union Army*, 1:293–94.
334. Smith, Camp and Barbour, *Record of Service of Connecticut Men*, 691.
335. Storrs, *"Twentieth Connecticut,"* 68.
336. *OR*, series I, vol. 27, part 1, 793–94.
337. American Civil War Research Database, "William W. Morse," Civil War Database.
338. Bailey, *Private Chapter of the War*, 238.
339. National Archives, Military Service Records, William W. Morse.
340. *Daily Morning Journal and Courier*, "Obituary Notes: Funeral of W.W. Morse To-day," 7.
341. *Morning Journal Courier*, "Death of W.W. Morse," 1.
342. *Daily Morning Journal and Courier*, "Funeral of W.W. Morse," 2; Find A Grave, William Wilson Morse (1837–1898).
343. National Archives and Records Administration, Pension Card Index, Morse, William W.
344. Treadwell, Darrah and Sell, *Photographers of the United States of America*, 257.
345. O'Brien and Diefendorf, *General Orders of the War Department*, 1:217.
346. Todd, *American Military Equipage*, 1:57–58.
347. U.S. War Department, *Revised United States Army Regulations of 1861*, 465–67.
348. Morhous, *Reminiscences of the 123rd Regiment*, 4–5, 7–8, 10, 12–16, 18.
349. Stewart, Holloway, Grierson and Pierce, *Union Army*, 2:139–40.
350. *OR*, series I, vol. 27, part 1, 797–99.
351. National Archives, Military Service Records, George W. Smith.
352. Morhous, *Reminiscences of the 123rd Regiment*, 199.
353. Historic.one, "Historical Marker: George Webster Smith."
354. *Texas Republican*, "Military Indictment Against Jefferson Prisoners," 1.
355. Find A Grave, George Webster Smith (1841–1868).
356. U.S. War Department, *Revised United States Army Regulations of 1861*, 468–69.
357. Todd, *American Military Equipage*, 1:178–79.
358. U.S. War Department, *Revised United States Army Regulations of 1861*, 465–66.
359. Todd, *American Military Equipage*, 1:57–58.
360. U.S. War Department, *Revised United States Army Regulations of 1861*, 472, 474.
361. National Archives, Military Service Records, Duncan Robertson.
362. FamilySearch, United States Census, 1860.
363. FamilySearch, United States Census, 1880, image 10 of 33.

364. *Post-Star*, "Veterans' Reunion," 3.

365. Find A Grave, Captain Duncan Robertson (1824–1899).

366. *Post-Star*, "Obituary," 4.

367. FamilySearch, New York, State Death Index, 1880–1956.

368. FamilySearch, United States General Index to Pension Files, 1861–1934.

369. U.S. War Department, *Revised United States Army Regulations of 1861*, 465.

370. Todd, *American Military Equipage*, 1:55–56.

371. U.S. War Department, *Revised United States Army Regulations of 1861*, 481.

372. Vernon and Wilmer, *History and Roster of Maryland Volunteers*, 110.

373. Stewart, Holloway, Grierson and Pierce, *Union Army*, 2:271–72.

374. Vernon and Wilmer, *History and Roster of Maryland Volunteers*, 111; Stewart, Holloway, Grierson and Pierce, *Union Army*, 2:272.

375. *OR*, series I, vol. 27, part 1, 795.

376. Ibid., 796–97.

377. *Yonkers Herald*, "Obituary," June 25, 1908, 2.

378. National Archives, Military Service Records, Gilbert P. Robinson.

379. FamilySearch, United States Census, 1880, image 18 of 95.

380. FamilySearch, United States Census, 1870; *Yonkers Herald*, "Obituary," June 25, 1908, 2.

381. *Yonkers Herald*, "Obituary," June 25, 1908, 2; *Jersey City News*, "Col. Robinson Honored," 2.

382. *Yonkers Herald*, "Obituary," June 25, 1908, 2; Find A Grave, Colonel Gilbert Proud Robinson (1831–1908).

383. U.S. War Department, *Revised United States Army Regulations of 1861*, 462–63.

384. Adjunct General's Office, *General Orders Affecting the Volunteer Forces*, 170.

385. U.S. War Department, *Revised United States Army Regulations of 1861*, 481.

Epilogue

386. Gottfried, *Brigades of Gettysburg*, 549–50.

387. Pfanz, *Gettysburg*, 285.

388. New York Monuments Commission, *Slocum and His Men*, 184–85.

389. Pfanz, *Gettysburg*, 352.

390. New York Monuments Commission, *Slocum and His Men*, 185.

Appendix

391. Busey and Martin, *Regimental Strengths and Losses at Gettysburg*, 101.

392. Ibid., 143.

393. Ibid., 157.

394. Ibid., 101.

395. Ibid., 143.

396. Ibid., 157.

397. Ibid., 101.

398. Ibid., 143.
399. Ibid., 157.
400. Ibid., 101.
401. Ibid., 143.
402. Ibid., 157.
403. Ibid., 99.
404. Ibid., 142.
405. Ibid., 157.
406. Ibid., 99.
407. Ibid., 142.
408. Ibid., 157.
409. Ibid., 99.
410. Ibid., 142.
411. Ibid., 157.
412. Ibid., 99.
413. Ibid., 142.
414. Ibid., 157.
415. Ibid., 98.
416. Ibid., 142.
417. Ibid., 157.
418. Ibid., 98.
419. Ibid., 142.
420. Ibid., 157.
421. Ibid., 98.
422. Ibid., 142.
423. Ibid., 157.
424. Ibid., 102.
425. Ibid., 143.
426. Ibid., 102.
427. Ibid., 96.
428. Ibid., 141.
429. Ibid., 156.
430. Ibid., 96.
431. Ibid., 141.
432. Ibid., 156.
433. Ibid., 96.
434. Ibid., 141.
435. Ibid., 156.
436. Ibid., 96.
437. Ibid., 141.
438. Ibid., 156.
439. Ibid., 96.
440. Ibid., 141.
441. Ibid., 156.

BIBLIOGRAPHY

Primary Sources

Adjunct General's Office. *General Orders Affecting the Volunteer Forces: 1864*. Washington, D.C.: Government Printing Office, 1865.

Adjutant General's Office. *Official Army Register for 1865*. Washington, D.C.: Government Printing Office, 1865.

Bailey, George W. *A Private Chapter of the War*. St. Louis, MO: G.I. Jones and Company, 1880.

Brown, Edmund Randolph. *The Twenty-Seventh Indiana Volunteer Infantry in the War of the Rebellion, 1861 to 1865*. Monticello, IN: Brown, 1899.

Carman, Ezra. *The Maryland Campaign of September 1862*. Vol. 1: *South Mountain*. Edited by Thomas Clemens. El Dorado Hills, CA: Savas Beatie, 2010.

Eddy, Richard. *History of the Sixtieth Regiment New York State Volunteers*. Philadelphia, PA: self-published, 1864.

Marvin, Edwin E. *The Fifth Regiment Connecticut Volunteers*. Hartford, CT: Press of Wiley, Waterman & Eaton, 1889.

Moody, John Sheldon, Calvin Duvall Cowles, Frederick Caryton Ainsworth et al. *The War of the Rebellion: A Compilation of the Official Records of the Union and Confederate Armies*. Series I, vol. 25, part 2. U.S. War Department. Washington, D.C.: Government Printing Office, 1889.

———. *The War of the Rebellion: A Compilation of the Official Records of the Union and Confederate Armies*. Series I, vol. 27, parts 1–3. U.S. War Department. Washington, D.C.: Government Printing Office, 1889.

Morhous, Henry C. *Reminiscences of the 123rd Regiment, N.Y.S.V. Giving a Complete History of Its Three Years' Service in the War*. Greenwich, NY: People's Journal Book & Job Office, 1879.

National Archives and Records Administration. Special Schedules of the Eleventh Census (1890) Enumerating Union Veterans and Widows of Union Veterans of the Civil War; Series Number: M123; Record Group Title: Records of the Department of Veterans Affairs; Record Group Number: 15; Census Year: 1890.

1910 Census. Place: Elmore Daviess, Indiana; Roll: T624_344; Page: 4A; Enumeration District: 0005; FHL microfilm: 1374357.

O'Brien, Thomas M., and Oliver Diefendorf. *General Orders of the War Department, Embracing the Years 1861, 1862 & 1863. Adapted Specifically for the Use of the Army and Navy of the United States.* Vols. 1 and 2. New York: Derby & Miller, 1864.

Orr, Timothy J., ed. *Last to Leave the Field: The Life and Letters of First Sergeant Ambrose Henry Hayward, 28th Pennsylvania Volunteers.* Knoxville: University of Tennessee Press, 2011.

Paver, John M. *What I Saw from 1861 to 1864.* Indianapolis, IN: Scott-Miller Company, 1906.

Quint, Alonzo H. *The Record of the Second Massachusetts Infantry, 1861–65.* Boston, MA: James P. Walker, 1867.

Records of the Department of Veterans Affairs. M123, Record Group Number: 15; Census Year: 1890.

Storrs, John W. *The "Twentieth Connecticut": A Regimental History.* Ansonia, CT: Naugatuck Valley Sentinel, 1886.

Tuttle, Russell M. *The Civil War Journal of Lt. Russell M. Tuttle, New York Volunteer Infantry.* Edited by George H. Tappan. Jefferson, NC: McFarland & Company, 2006.

U.S. War Department. *Revised Regulations for the Army of the United States, 1861. With a Full Index.* Philadelphia, PA: George W. Childs, 1862.

———. *Revised United States Army Regulations of 1861, with an Appendix Containing the Changed and Laws Affecting Army Regulations and Articles of War to June 25, 1863.* Washington, D.C.: Government Printing Office, 1863.

Weller, Edwin. *A Civil War Courtship: The Letters of Edwin Weller from Antietam to Atlanta.* Edited by William Walton. Garden City, NY: Doubleday & Company Inc., 1980.

Wilson, Lawrence. *Itinerary of the Seventh Ohio Volunteer Infantry, 1861–1864.* New York: Neale Publishing Company, 1907.

Newspapers

Boonville Enquirer. "Short Treasurers." December 25, 1886, 2.

Boston Globe. "Dorchester District." May 7, 1920, 11.

———. "Funeral of Maj John A. Fox Tomorrow Afternoon." May 6, 1920, 16.

———. "A Striking Story." July 25, 1876, 8.

Boston Post. "At the Point of Pines." August 29, 1881, 1.

Buffalo Evening News. "Dr. Scott W. Skinner Dies at Le Roy." July 23, 1927, 3.

Butte Inter Mountain. "Sale of Purebred Stock in Helena on May 6." March 25, 1903, 3.

Chicago Daily Tribune. "Van Buren." April 25, 1921, 19.

Cleveland Daily Leader. "The Funeral." December 8, 1863, 3.

———. "Public Proceedings in Honor of Colonel William R. Creighton and Lieut. Col. Crane." December 3, 1863, 3.

Daily Morning Journal and Courier. "Funeral of W.W. Morse." December 9, 1998, 2.

———. "Obituary Notes: Funeral of W.W. Morse To-day." December 8, 1898, 7.

Democrat & Chronicle. "Dr. Skinner, 83, Noted Le Roy Surgeon, Dies." July 23, 1927, 3.

Great Falls Tribune. "Pensions for Montanans." May 27, 1902, 5.

Harrisburg Daily Independent. "Captain Spink Dead." August 8, 1912, 7.

Harrisburg Telegraph. "Captain Spink Victim of Cancer." August 8, 1912, 3.

———. "Full Military Honors for Late Capt. Spink." August 10, 1912, 9.

Hartford Courant. "The 107th New York Regiment." August 18, 1862, 2.

Independent-Record. "George W.P. Pew Dead." June 11, 1904, 5.

Indianapolis Journal. "Indiana Notes." December 1, 1892, 5.

———. "The Martin County Auditorship." November 25, 1886, 2.

Jersey City News. "Col. Robinson Honored." May 22, 1900, 2.

La Crosse Tribune. "Retired Merchant, 89, Is Dead at Janesville." March 9, 1930, 14.

Lancaster Examiner. "A Soldier's Suicide." May 25, 1887, 3.

Mansfield Advisor. "Chemung County." September 12, 1888, 2.

Marion (OH) Star. "Burials." October 19, 1899, 8.

———. "Captain Watkins." September 21, 1899, 4.

Martin County Democrat. "The Recount Concluded." November 26, 1886, 1.

Morning Journal Courier. "Death of W.W. Morse." December 6, 1898, 1.

New York Daily Herald. "The Late Major Gilbert M. Elliott." December 10, 1863, 5.

Philadelphia Enquirer. "Earnest Goodman Suddenly Expires." February 4, 1896, 7.

———. "The Loyal Legion." February 6, 1890, 3.

———. "A Quarrel Between Partners." January 29, 1880, 2.

Philadelphia Times. "Dr. Goodman's Fatal Run." February 6, 1896, 2.

———. "An Old Soldier's Suicide." May 20, 1887, 1.

Post-Star. "Obituary." August 3, 1899, 4.

———. "The Veterans' Reunion." August 21, 1884, 3.

Star-Gazette. "Capt. Frank P. Frost." November 5, 1934, 17.

———. "Capt. Frank P. Frost." November 6, 1934, 6.

———. "Edwin G. Fay." June 14, 1902, 5.

———. "Edwin G. Fry." June 16, 1902, 7.

———. "Just Chat." November 5, 1934, 3.

———. "107th N.Y. VOLS." September 17, 1896, 5, 7.

———. "Personal." September 17, 1896, 7.

———. "Taps Sound for Captain Frank P. Frost." November 5, 1934, 5.

Texas Republican. "Military Indictment Against Jefferson Prisoners." May 28, 1869, 1.

York Dispatch. "Captain Spink." August 8, 1912, 8.

Military Service Records

National Archives, Military Service Records. Alexander, John, Company B, 5th Connecticut Infantry.

———. Crane, Orrin J., Field & Staff, 7th Ohio Infantry.

———. Creighton, William R., Field & Staff, 7th Ohio Infantry.

———. Diven, Eugene, Company A, 60th New York Infantry.

————. Donovan, Michael, Company D, 5th Connecticut Infantry.

————. Fay, Edwin G., Company C, 107th New York Infantry.

————. Fox, John A., Company H, 46th Pennsylvania Infantry.

————. Frost, Frank, Company D, 107th New York Infantry.

————. Gaither, Wilson B., Company B, 5th Ohio Infantry.

————. Goodman, Henry E., Field & Staff, 28th Pennsylvania Infantry.

————. Elliot, Gilbert Molleson, Company E, 102nd New York Infantry.

————. Morse, William W., Company G, 20th Connecticut Infantry.

————. Pew, George W., Company H, 137th New York Infantry.

————. Ragle, Peter, Jr., Company B, 27th Indiana Infantry.

————. Robertson, Duncan, Company F, 123rd New York Infantry.

————. Robinson, Gilbert P., Company C, 3rd Maryland Infantry.

————. Schuck, Martin H., Battery B, 1st New York Light Artillery.

————. Schwab, Mathias, Company K, 5th Ohio Infantry.

————. Scofield, William A., Company F, 137th New York Infantry.

————. Selfridge, James L., Field and Staff, 46th Pennsylvania Infantry.

————. Skinner, Scott, Company G, 78th New York Infantry.

————. Smith, George W., Company B, 123rd New York Infantry.

————. Spink, Arnold B., Company I, 28th Pennsylvania Infantry.

————. Van Buren, Barent, Company F, 102nd New York Infantry.

————. Watkins, John W., Company E, 66th Ohio Infantry.

————. Winslow, Frederick, Company I, 60th New York Infantry.

Secondary Sources

Bates, Samuel P. *History of Pennsylvania Volunteers, 1861–1865.* Vols. 1–5. Harrisburg, PA: B. Singerly, State Printer, 1869–70.

Busey, John W., and David G. Martin. *Regimental Strengths and Losses at Gettysburg.* 4th ed. N.p.: Longstreet House, Hightstown, New Jersey Rouge, 2005.

Clark, Gary W. *19th Century Card Photos Kwik Guide: A Step-by-Step Guide to Identifying and Dating Cartes de Vistite and Cabinet Cards.* Wichita, KS: PhotoTree, 2013.

Cleutz, David. *Fields of Fame & Glory: Col. David Ireland and the 137th New York Volunteers.* Bloomington, IN: Xlibris, 2010.

Coffin, Selden J. *Record of the Men of Lafayette: Brief Biographical Sketches of the Alumni of Lafayette College.* Easton, PA: Skinner & Finch, 1879.

Darrah, William C. *Cartes de Visite: In Nineteenth Century Photography.* Gettysburg, PA: W.C. Darrah Publisher, 1981.

Debevoise, Dickinson R., ed. *Gilbert Molleson Elliott: A Life Forged in the Crucible of the American Experience.* Spartanburg, SC: Reprint Company, 2002.

Dyer, Frederick H. *A Compendium of the War of the Rebellion.* Vol. 3, *Regimental Histories.* Des Moines, IA: F.H. Dyer, 1908.

Fox, William F. *New York at Gettysburg.* Vol. 3. Albany, NY: J.B. Lyon Company, 1900.

Gottfried, Bradley M. *Brigades of Gettysburg: The Union and Confederate Brigades at the Battle of Gettysburg.* New York: Skyhorse Publishing, 2012.

————. *The Maps of Gettysburg: An Atlas to the Gettysburg Campaign, June 3–July 1, 1863*. El Dorado Hills, CA: Savas Beatie, 2007.

Hunt, Roger D. *Colonels in Blue: Michigan, Ohio and West Virginia*. Jefferson, NC: McFarland & Company, 2011.

Lord, Francis A. *Civil War Collector's Encyclopedia*. Secaucus, NJ: Castle, 1982.

Monument Committee. *Fifth Connecticut Volunteers Dedication Excursion and Reunion, at Gettysburg, August 8th, 9th, and 10th, 1887*. Hartford, CT: Press of Wiley, Waterman & Eaton, 1887.

New York Monuments Commission for the Battlefields of Gettysburg, Chattanooga and Antietam. *Slocum and His Men*. Albany, NY: J.B. Lyon Company, 1904.

Nicholson, John P. *Re-Union of the 28th & 147th Regiments, Pennsylvania Volunteers, Philadelphia, Nov. 24th, 1871*. Philadelphia, PA: Pawson & Nicholson, 1872.

Peckham, Harriett C. Waite Van Buren. *History of Cornelis Maessen Van Buren*. New York: Tobias A. Wright, Printer & Publisher, 1913.

Pfanz, Harry W. *Gettysburg: Culp's Hill and Cemetery Hill*. Chapel Hill: University of North Carolina Press, 1993.

Phisterer, Frederick. *New York in the War of the Rebellion, 1861 to 1865*. Albany, NY: Weed, Parsons & Company, 1890.

Reid, Whitelaw. *Ohio in the War: Her Statesmen, Her Generals, and Soldiers*. Vol. 2. Cincinnati, OH: Moore, Wilstach & Baldwin, 1868.

Smith, Stephen R., Frederick E. Camp and Lucius A. Barbour. *Record of Service of Connecticut Men in the Army and Navy of the United States during the War of the Rebellion*. Hartford, CT: Case, Lockwood & Brainard Company, 1889.

Stewart, James, Jr., William R. Holloway, Benjamin H. Grierson and Byron Root Pierce. *The Union Army*. Vols. 1–10. Wilmington, NC: Broadfoot, 1997. First published in 1908 by Federal Publishing Company.

Tice, Warren K. *Uniform Buttons of the United States, 1776–1865*. Gettysburg, PA: Thomas Publications, 1997.

Todd, Frederick P. *American Military Equipage, 1851–1872*. Vol. 1. Providence, RI: Company of Military Historians, 1974.

Treadwell, T.K., William C. Darrah and Wolfgang Sell. *Photographers of the United States of America*. N.p.: National Stereoscopic Association, 1994. Updated edition, 2003.

Vernon, George W.F., and J.H. Jarrett Wilmer. *History and Roster of Maryland Volunteers, War of 1861–65*. Baltimore, MD: Press of Guggenheimer, Weil & Company, 1898.

Warner, Ezra J. *Generals in Blue: Lives of the Union Commanders*. Baton Rouge: Louisiana State University Press, 2006.

Woodhead, Henry, ed. *Echoes of Glory: Arms and Equipment of the Union*. Alexandria, VA: Time-Life Books, 1991.

Primary Source Websites

American Civil War Research Database. "Personnel Directory" and "Regimental Lookup." Consulted regularly throughout writing. http://www.civilwardata.com/active/pers_dir.html.

Ancestry. *1870 United States Federal Census*. Provo, UT: Ancestry.com Operations Inc., 2009.

———. *New York, U.S., State Census, 1875*. Provo, UT: Ancestry.com Operations Inc., 2013.

———. *Ohio, U.S., County Marriage Records, 1774–1993*. Lehi, UT: Ancestry.com Operations Inc., 2016.

———. *U.S., City Directories, 1822–1995*. Lehi, UT: Ancestry.com Operations Inc., 2011.

Antietam on the Web. Consulted throughout writing. http://antietam.aotw.org/index.php.

Cincinnati Fire Department History. "Captain Mathias Schwab." http://www.cfdhistory.com/htmls/loddind.php?info=12.

Civil War Veterans. "Ragle, Peter." Daviess County InGenWeb. Last updated December 30, 2010. http://ingenmdb.org/indiana/military/civilVets.html#

FamilySearch. California, County Birth and Death Records, 1800–1994. Database with images, March 1, 2021, Michael Donovan, 1929. https://familysearch.org/ark:/61903/1:1:QGLS-5VX4.

———. New York, State Death Index, 1880–1956, database. https://familysearch.org/ark:/61903/3:1:3Q9M-CSG8-R9WP-1?cc=2803479.

———. New York, State Death Index, 1880–1956, database. Martin H. Schuck, 1915. https://www.familysearch.org/ark:/61903/1:1:QG2T-19PK.

———. United States Census of Union Veterans and Widows of the Civil War, 1890. https://familysearch.org/ark:/61903/3:1:939V-5NP8-4?cc=1877095&wc=M62D-GMW%3A174324501%2C174725501%2C174320903, Pennsylvania > Juniata > All > image 59 of 63, citing NARA microfilm publication M123. Washington, D.C.: National Archives and Records Administration, n.d.

———. United States Census, 1860. A. Spinck, 1860. https://familysearch.org/ark:/61903/1:1:MXPZ-9P3.

———. United States Census, 1860. https://familysearch.org/ark:/61903/3:1:33S7-9BSC-QKH?cc=1473181&wc=7Q5P-MFH%3A1589422212%2C1589422318%2C1589428884, New York > Washington > Argyle > image 55 of 76, from "1860 U.S. Federal Census—Population," database, Fold3. http://www.fold3.com. Citing NARA microfilm publication M653. Washington, D.C.: National Archives and Records Administration, n.d.

———. United States Census, 1870. https://familysearch.org/ark:/61903/3:1:S3HT-XCSC-N85?cc=1438024&wc=KG43-929%3A518652701%2C519218601%2C519314401, New Jersey > Hudson > Jersey City, ward 11 > image 156 of 184, citing NARA microfilm publication M593. Washington, D.C.: National Archives and Records Administration, n.d.

———. United States Census, 1880. https://familysearch.org/ark:/61903/3:1:33S7-9YBG-NSG?cc=1417683&wc=XH8F-829%3A1589409304%2C1589410674%2C1589401875%2C1589396176, New York > Niagara > Lockport > ED 182 > image 30 of 35, citing NARA microfilm publication T9. National Archives and Records Administration, Washington, D.C., n.d.

———. United States Census, 1880. https://familysearch.org/ark:/61903/3:1:33SQGYBK-YBH?cc=1417683&wc=XZ33-N38%3A1589408696%2C1589408898%2C1589408897%2C1589394791, New Jersey > Hudson > Jersey City > ED 26 > image 18 of 95, citing NARA microfilm publication T9. National Archives and Records Administration, Washington, D.C., n.d.

———. United States Census, 1880. https://familysearch.org/ark:/61903/3:1:33S7-9YBV-96X1?cc=1417683&wc=XCPJ-ZNL%3A1589409304%2C1589395180%2C1589405474%2C1589394977, New York > Washington > Argyle > ED 128 > image 10 of 33, citing NARA microfilm publication T9. National Archives and Records Administration, Washington, D.C., n.d.

———. United States Census, 1900. Edwin G. Fay, 1900. Last updated January 13, 2022. https://www.familysearch.org/ark:/61903/1:1:M3WH-VYD.

———. United States General Index to Pension Files, 1861–1934. https://familysearch.org/ark:/61903/3:1:33SQ-GT1Z-W1H?cc=1919699&wc=9FFT-3TL%3A214220601, Roberts, George F.—Robilliard, John > image 3155 of 4511, citing NARA microfilm publication T288. Washington, D.C.: National Archives and Records Administration, n.d.

Fold3. New York Civil War Muster Roll Abstracts. Last modified 2014. https://www.fold3.com/image/315773469?terms=skinner,war,us,civil,union,united,america,scott,states.

———. New York Civil War Muster Roll Abstracts. Last modified 2014. https://www.fold3.com/image/315869227.

———. New York Civil War Muster Roll, 1861–1900, 867 and 869. https://www.fold3.com/image/315987095.

General Information about the Ohio Girls Industrial School. Last updated September 22, 2022. https://ohiohistory.libguides.com/c.php?g=1110058&p=8092330.

Historic.one. "Historical Marker: George Webster Smith." https://historic.one/tx/marion-county/historical-marker/george-webster-smith#gsc.tab=0.

Historic Marker Database. "Field Hospitals—Twelfth Corps Medical Department—Army of the Potomac." Last revised November 30, 2020. https://www.hmdb.org/m.asp?m=17924.

Massachusetts Historical Society. "Fox Family Papers." Last updated 2005. https://www.masshist.org/collection-guides/view/fa0158.

National Archives and Records Administration, Compiled Service Records. Civil War Service Records (CMSR)—Union—Massachusetts—Fold3, pages 3, 17.

National Archives and Records Administration, Pension Card Index. Alexander, John, Civil War Pensions Index—Fold3.

———. Crane, Orrin J., Civil War Pensions Index—Fold3.

———. Diven, Eugene, Civil War Pensions Index—Fold 3.

———. Donovan, Michael, Civil War Pensions Index—Fold3.

———. Fay, Edwin G., Civil War Pensions Index—Fold3.

———. Fox, John A., Civil War Pensions Index—Fold3.

———. Frost, Frank P., Civil War Pensions Index—Fold3.

———. Gaither, Wilson B., Civil War Pensions Index—Fold3.

————. Heath, William H., Civil War Pensions Index—Fold3.

————. Mann, Albert W., Civil War Pensions Index—Fold3.

————. Morse, William W., Civil War Pensions Index—Fold3.

————. Pew, George W.P., Civil War Pensions Index—Fold3.

————. Ragle, Peter, Civil War Pensions Index—Fold3.

————. Schuck, Martin H., Civil War Pensions Index—Fold3.

————. Scofield, William A., Civil War Pensions Index—Fold3.

————. Selfridge, James L., Civil War Pensions Index—Fold3.

————. Van Buren, Barent, Civil War Pensions Index—Fold3.

————. Watkins, John W., Civil War Pensions Index—Fold3.

————. Winslow, Frederick S., Civil War Pensions Index—Fold3.

Pennsylvania in the Civil War Database. 126th Regiment Pennsylvania Volunteers. pa-roots.com.

————. 129th Regiment Pennsylvania Volunteers. pa-roots.com.

————. 131st Regiment Pennsylvania Volunteers. pa-roots.com.

————. 91st Regiment Pennsylvania Volunteers. pa-roots.com.

Rootsweb. "The Trueblood Family in America." Last updated February 16, 2004. https://freepages.rootsweb.com/~dbeeler/genealogy/fam/fam04198.html.

Secondary Source Websites

Find A Grave. Consulted regularly throughout writing. https://www.findagrave.com.

Index

Military Units

C

ABOUT THE AUTHORS

A longtime student of American history and the Civil War, MATTHEW BORDERS holds a BA in U.S. history and an MS in historic preservation. He has worked as a National Park Service ranger at Antietam National Battlefield, as well as a historian and battlefield surveyor for the National Park Service's American Battlefield Protection Program. He is also a Certified Battlefield Guide at Antietam and Harpers Ferry. Matthew is a founding member of the Antietam Institute, as well as a member of the Save Historic Antietam Foundation (SHAF) and the president of the Frederick County Civil War Round Table. Currently, he is a National Park Service ranger at Monocacy National Battlefield in Frederick, Maryland. Along with fellow Antietam guide and coauthor Joe Stahl, he continues to research and expand on the *Faces of Union Soldiers* series.

JOSEPH W. STAHL retired from the Institute for Defense Analyses, where he authored or coauthored more than fifty reports on defense issues. Since his retirement, he has become a volunteer and NPS Licensed Battlefield Guide at Antietam and Harpers Ferry. He grew up in St. Louis. He received BS and MS degrees from Missouri University of Science and Technology and an MBA from Washington University

in St. Louis. He is a member of the Company of Military Historians, the Antietam Institute, the Save Historic Antietam Foundation (SHAF) and the Hagerstown Civil War Round Table. He has spoken to various Civil War groups, including the Northern Virginia Relic Hunters; South Mountain Coin and Relic Club; Rappahannock, York, Chambersburg and Hagerstown Round Tables; Chambersburg Civil War Tours; SHAF; and NPS Antietam. In addition, Joe has authored more than two dozen articles about items in his collections for *Gettysburg Magazine*, the *Washington Times* Civil War Page, *Manuscripts*, *America's Civil War*, *Military Collector & Historian* (the journal of the Company of Military Historians), the *Civil War Historian* and the *Skirmish Line* of the North-South Skirmish Association. Displays of items from his collection have won awards at several Civil War shows. He has been a member of the North-South Skirmish Association for more than twenty-five years and has shot Civil War–type muskets, carbines and revolvers in both individual and team competitions.

Visit us at
www.historypress.com